Neighbourhoods on the net

T0324236

Neighbourhoods on the net: The nature and impact of internet-based neighbourhood information systems

Roger Burrows, Nick Ellison and Brian Woods

JOSEPH ROWNTREE
FOUNDATION

First published in Great Britain in July 2005 by

The Policy Press
Fourth Floor, Beacon House
Queen's Road
Bristol BS8 1QU
UK

Tel no +44 (0)117 331 4054
Fax no +44 (0)117 331 4093
Email tpp-info@bristol.ac.uk
www.policypress.org.uk

Published for the Joseph Rowntree Foundation by The Policy Press

ISBN 1 86134 771 5

British Library Cataloguing in Publication Data
A catalogue record for this book is available from the British Library.

Library of Congress Cataloging-in-Publication Data
A catalog record for this book has been requested.

Roger Burrows is Professor of Sociology in the Department of Sociology at the University of York, UK. He has research interests in housing, neighbourhoods and the sociology of place, health and illness, and social informatics.
Nick Ellison is a Senior Lecturer in the School of Applied Social Sciences at the University of Durham, UK. He has research interests in comparative social policy, citizenship, and the emerging social politics of place. **Brian Woods** is a Research Fellow in the Science and Technology Studies Unit in the Department of Sociology at the University of York, UK. He has research interests in social studies of science and technology, the social history of wheelchairs and disability, and aspects of health, illness and the body.

The **Joseph Rowntree Foundation** has supported this project as part of its programme of research and innovative development projects, which it hopes will be of value to policy makers, practitioners and service users. The facts presented and views expressed in this report are, however, those of the authors and not necessarily those of the Foundation.

The statements and opinions contained within this publication are solely those of the authors and not of The University of Bristol or The Policy Press. The University of Bristol and The Policy Press disclaim responsibility for any injury to persons or property resulting from any material published in this publication.

The Policy Press works to counter discrimination on grounds of gender, race, disability, age and sexuality.

Cover design by Qube Design Associates, Bristol
Printed in Great Britain by Hobbs the Printers Ltd, Southampton

Contents

Acknowledgements

Thanks are due to:

- Maz Hardey and Hannes Hansen-Magnusson, for research assistance on this project;
- Theresa McDonagh at the Joseph Rowntree Foundation, for continuing support and enthusiasm for our work;
- all members of our Project Advisory Group – Ben Anderson, Nick Bailey, Leonard Waverman, Dev Virdee, Helen Triggs, Derek Long and Richard Webber – even though not all of them will agree with what we have to say;
- all those we interviewed as part of the project, especially those in California, Oregon and Vancouver who made our stay so pleasant and productive – Nick Gane, Bert Sperling and Thomas Kempner in particular;
- Howard Cambridge from the Stockholm Environment Institute at York for helpful technical comment; and finally
- Mike Hardey, Brian Loader, Andrew Webster, Graham Lewis and Sarah Nettleton for their interest and support.

Executive summary

Chapter 1: Neighbourhood images in the information age

Images of neighbourhoods influence both the lives of the people who reside in them and the attitudes and behaviours of others. Whereas these images were once generated fairly locally, the ongoing information revolution means that detailed internet-sourced 'local knowledge' is becoming freely available at various levels of detail. The nature and potential impact of what are referred to here as *internet-based neighbourhood information systems* are the focus of this report.

Chapter 2: New forms of local knowledge? The emergence of internet-based neighbourhood information systems

Internet usage has increased exponentially in recent years, reaching more than 800 million users globally in 2004. In Euro-American societies it is now a technology to which the majority have access. Despite this, various forms of 'digital divide' still exist. Such divides refer both to unequal patterns of access to the technology *and* to the manner in which the technology itself can be used to divide populations. This report maps out some of the potential costs and benefits that technologies associated with providing online information about communities and neighbourhoods might possess.

We examine internet sites that offer *free access* to various sorts of *searchable spatially referenced data* (statistical and qualitative). Key sites are identified and are classified into four main types: *commercial*; *geodemographic*; *policy and research*; and *social software*. Brief details of these sites are listed together with some more detailed 'snapshots' of a subsample of key providers.

Chapter 3: Four case studies

Four exemplar case studies of internet-based neighbourhood information systems are examined, each relating to our fourfold typology, two from the UK and two from the US: upmystreet.com; houseandhome.msn.com; neighbourhood.statistics.gov.uk; and scorecard.org.

Chapter 4: Some theoretical perspectives

This chapter examines recent academic research that has focused on the relationship between physical urban spaces and digital technologies. Internet-based neighbourhood information systems (IBNIS) are a cluster of technologies that clearly operate at this interface and, as such, provide a good test case for exploring some of the theoretical claims made in this literature. We examine IBNIS in the light of claims that they could be functioning as pieces of *social sorting software*. We conclude that this could well be the case (especially in the future) but that, as yet, there is not enough empirical evidence to assess this claim one way or another.

Chapter 5: Key stakeholder perspectives

Following on from this conceptual consideration of internet-based neighbourhood information systems (IBNIS), we next examine the views of a range of stakeholders involved in the production and consumption of the technology. Twenty exploratory 'conversational interviews' were conducted with stakeholders ranging from geodemographic software developers, through front-line commercial and policy providers to homebuyers engaged in residential search. Among the different views about the nature and impact of IBNIS that were expressed, three features stand out:

1. the concern that many front-line companies have with information accuracy;
2. the enthusiasm – particularly in the UK – for IBNIS and the potential for further exploitation and development; and
3. differing perceptions of, and optimism about, IBNIS on the two sides of the Atlantic.

Chapter 6: Conclusions and implications for policy

If information *per se* (especially when it is free) is a 'good thing' because of its potential for producing more reflexive and detailed 'local knowledge', this potential can only be realised within a more 'equitable' policy framework that counteracts the potential tendency of internet-based neighbourhood information systems to 'software sort' and 'segment' populations (especially already disadvantaged populations).

Neighbourhood images in the information age

Introduction

Recent research (Cattell and Evans, 1999; Forrest and Kearns, 1999; Wood and Vamplew, 1999; Dean and Hastings, 2000; Silburn et al, 1999) has shown that the *images* that neighbourhoods possess can have a fundamental influence both on the lives of the people who currently reside within them, and on the attitudes and behaviours of various other groups and individuals with the power and influence to invoke change. This report argues that in a world where information and communication technologies of various sorts have become so important (Castells, 2000), the sources of such imagery are fundamentally changing (Westwood and Williams, 1997; Forrest, 2003). It is our contention that *everyday (more proximate and immanent) perceptions of place and local identity* are – in many neighbourhoods – losing much of their influence. Not so long ago, images and perceptions of neighbourhoods and communities were generated from a range of primarily *local* sources. Local residents and those living nearby would be key 'information holders' about the history and folklore of local spaces, much of which was verbally communicated. Depictions of neighbourhoods were also the province of a range of local actors – estate agents, journalists, social workers and shopkeepers to name a few – who disseminated or 'spread' local knowledge for specific purposes in specific ways, distilling and perpetuating particular neighbourhood images as they did so. Of course, these means of generating local knowledge continue to exist, but times have changed, and, crucially, the *technological* means by which neighbourhood images are now constructed, disseminated and consumed have undergone nothing short of a revolution in recent years – and this revolution is ongoing.

Only a few years ago geographic information systems were "obscure technological systems requiring large computers, producing execrable output and interesting only a small few" (Curry, 1998, p 1). Today any member of the public with access to the internet and the inclination can quickly gain huge amounts of detailed geographically referenced information. For the most part, this internet-supplied *local knowledge* comes free and is available at various levels of spatial detail (sometimes termed 'granularity'). Moreover, it covers an expanding range of topics and comes in a format that (for the most part) requires no special training to interpret. In this report, we examine the emergence of what, following Krouk et al (2000), we term *internet-based neighbourhood information systems* (IBNIS).

Some examples of internet-based neighbourhood information systems

The best way to introduce the phenomena of IBNIS is to begin by getting a sense of the kind of local knowledge and thus neighbourhood imagery that can now be obtained via the internet. A couple of locations in the UK and the US illustrate very clearly what is already 'out there'. Consider, first, the neighbourhood defined by the postcode YO30 6WP – an area in York in the Yorkshire and Humber region of England – in which the headquarters of the Joseph Rowntree Foundation is located.

At www.upmystreet.com (UMS)[1], we discover that this area is classified (using a geodemographic system called ACORN©,

---

[1] We will examine this and the other websites we mention in this introduction in far more detail later on in the report.

Figure 1.1: House price trends data for YO30 6 derived from UMS website

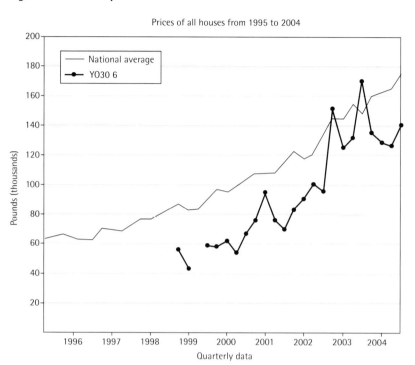

Prices of all houses from 1995 to 2004

discussed below) as a neighbourhood characterised as *older professionals in detached houses and apartments*. On the UMS website, such neighbourhoods are described as follows:

> ... affluent people living in largely suburban areas. Households tend to be a mixture of couples, families and singles, but with fewer children and more retired people than the UK as a whole. People tend to be well educated, and employed in senior managerial and professional occupations. Property is a mixture of houses and flats. The houses tend to be large, with four or more bedrooms, with slightly more semi-detached than detached and terraced. Flats are a mixture of purpose built and converted, some of which are privately rented. Reflecting the slightly older age profile of the people in this type, more of the houses are owned outright. Car ownership is high with two cars being very common. One of the cars is likely to be a high value company car. These affluent individuals have high incomes as well as high levels of savings and investments. They are also characterised by high credit card limits and high credit card usage. They make investments using financial advisers and brokers, as well as directly using the Internet. Internet

banking is very common. All the major broadsheets are read, and interests include fine arts and antiques, theatre and good food and wine. Eating out is also popular.

The UMS site also reports current house prices for the postcode using data from the Land Registry. In November 2004, a semi-detached house in YO30 6 cost an average of £156,440 compared with a national average of £157,767. It is also possible to produce graphs showing the recent history of house price movements such as the one reproduced in Figure 1.1.

At www.ourproperty.co.uk, even more detailed data from the Land Registry is available. After a short registration process, it is possible to download the actual price that individual properties have been sold for since April 2000[2]. Eight properties have been sold in this postcode since this date, some more than once. So, for example, one semi-detached house was sold on 20 September 2002 for £162,500 and then sold again on 5 September 2003 for £202,500 (an increase of almost 25% in less than 12 months,

---

[2] Similar data are also available via www.mouseprice.co.uk but unlike www.ourproperty.co.uk this site only provides data on a price-per-view basis. Since this chapter was first written UMS has introduced similar data, accessible following a short registration process.

although we do not know whether any improvements or changes had been made to the property). Another terraced property in the same street was sold for £187,000 on 26 June 2001 and sold again on 14 March 2003 for £395,00 (a 111% price increase in less than two years).

Returning to UMS and a few more clicks of the mouse and one can discover the nearest primary and secondary schools (one can then easily link to school websites, reports from the Office for Standards in Education and local school 'league tables'). More clicks and one can discover the distance of the centre of the postcode to a wide range of services: from York railway station through to local homeopaths, fish and chip shops, child minders, estate agents and so on). A few further clicks and one can read or participate in a series of asynchronous virtual 'conversations' about various aspects of York and its environs. People are posting messages to ask for 'local lay knowledge' about where to rent or buy accommodation, the quality of particular schools, the safety of particular cycle paths through the city, where to leave cats and dogs while on holiday and so on.

At www.homecheck.co.uk, information about the physical attributes of the neighbourhood can be found: the postcode is evidently 500 metres away from an indicative flood plain; the risks associated with subsidence, coal mines, landfill, pollution, and historical industrial land use are all judged to be high; but the risks from radon gas are judged to be low.

At www.statistics.gov.uk, access to a range of 'official' neighbourhood statistics can be obtained. It takes just a few mouse clicks to discover that the postcode is in the Clifton ward of the city (population 12,017 in 2001), which is ranked 2,469th (out of 8,414) most deprived in England[3]. Ward-level data on the population are also available and can be compared with York and England as a whole. The gender, age, household type, ethnic and religious make-up of the population is readily available, as are data concerned with health, caring responsibilities, economic activity, benefit claimants, students and

their qualifications, tenure, housing conditions and types, crime and much more. So, for example: 97.3% of the Clifton ward is classified as being 'White'; 67.8% as 'Christian' and 19.7% as possessing 'no religion'; 8.9% describe their health as 'not good'; 17.3% live with a limiting long-term illness; and 3.8% are 'unemployed'. Also available is an impressive interactive map that allows the user to 'drill down' to the level of individual streets and houses (although most data are only available across far larger geographic areas).

Such IBNIS have a slightly longer history in the US and tend to offer more detail and a greater capacity to search for neighbourhoods with particular combinations of attributes than is (so far) possible in the UK. Consider, by way of example, a neighbourhood defined by a zip code in Portland, Oregon, in the Pacific North West of the US – 97204 – a neighbourhood that contains the City of Portland *Office of Neighbourhood Involvement* (ONI), providers of a local city-wide IBNIS. ONI is based in the South West 4th Avenue area of downtown Portland, part of the Multnomah County. The site that ONI itself runs – www.portlandonline.com/oni – allows members of the public to use an elegant online map in order to view local data on: property; neighbourhoods; schools; parks; physical geography; crime; and much more. This mapping can be done at various levels of detail ranging from particular addresses right the way up to the city boundary itself. Much of the data can be organised not just via administrative boundaries and the various types of areas used to gather census information but also via 95 neighbourhood association zones that, it is claimed, residents themselves perceive as having a high degree of social and cultural integrity.

At houseandhome.msn.com one can obtain detailed demographic data on zip code 97204. The population is 1,742 people living in 666 households with a median household income of $26,221 (well below both the regional and the national average). The median age is 35.3 and 74% of the population is male. Other detailed information is available that relates to: educational levels; crime; cost of living; health and safety; employment; housing; and transportation. It is also possible to compare the characteristics of this zip code with others in other parts of the country in order to ascertain which provide the closest 'match'. So, for

---

3   Using the 2000 version of the Office of the Deputy Prime Minister's Indices of Multiple Deprivation (IMD). Data are also available on the site using the 2004 IMD and these are organised at a more detailed Census 'super output area' level of detail.

instance, if one compares 97204 with zip codes in Massachusetts, the nearest matches are revealed as 02215 in Boston and 022465 in West Newton.

My Best Segments – a website run by geodemographers Claritas Inc – provides data for every zip code in the US based on a number of its system of geodemographic classification. Using its PRIZM$_{NE}$© classification, for example, the most common socio-demographic segments living within zip code 97204 are revealed to be those categorised as *low-rise living* – described as the most economically challenged urban segment, young ethnically diverse singles and single parents – and *urban elders* – described as older Hispanics and African-Americans living in downtown areas as singles in older apartment rentals.

At www.scorecard.org, one is able to generate a highly detailed pollution report on every zip code in the US. For zip code 97204 – Multnomah – it is revealed that in 2002 the area ranked among the "dirtier 30% of all counties in the US in terms of air releases of recognized developmental toxicants". A list of the main polluters is provided; topping this list are Wacker Siltronic Corp, Dynea Overlays Inc and Columbia Stell Castings Co Inc. The main pollutants in the area include: nitrate compounds (1,074,401 pounds); methanol (225,681); manganese compounds (200,112); and ammonia (74,715).

Structure of the report

In order to scope the significance of such IBNIS, we have: examined in detail a representative range of IBNIS; read what has been written about them, their background and the broader context of their emergence; interviewed a number of stakeholders involved in the development and use of such systems in both the UK and the US; and considered what we have learnt from these three sources in the context of broader conceptual and policy interests in the differentiated social politics of neighbourhood life that is emerging in the early 21st century.

In the next chapter, we place the emergence of IBNIS within the context of broader discussions of the impact the internet is having on everyday life and also attempt to define more precisely what we intend by the notion of IBNIS. We then produce a simple typology of different types of IBNIS and briefly describe an illustrative sample of different sites using this typology. In the third chapter, we examine four exemplar IBNIS in more detail. The fourth chapter offers a critical review of research literature that impinges upon the analysis of IBNIS. The fifth compares and contrasts this literature with the perspectives of a number of key stakeholders involved in the development and use of IBNIS. The final chapter offers a brief summary of our conclusions and points towards a range of possible policy implications.

New forms of local knowledge?
The emergence of internet-based neighbourhood information systems

The internet and everyday life

The emergence of internet-based neighbourhood information systems (IBNIS) has to be understood within the broader context of debates concerning the impact of the internet on everyday life. Although the origins of the internet can be traced back to (at least) the late 1960s (Abbate, 1999), it only really entered popular consciousness in the early 1990s, and it was only a decade ago that use of the technology began to register as a significant socio-cultural development in the media, the academy and at the level of policy. In 1995, there were only 16 million users of the internet across the globe (about 0.4% of the world population)[4]. By 2000, this figure had reached 451 million (7.4%) and by mid-2004 it stood at 812 million (12.7% of the adult population of the world).

Given the gross inequities of the global economic system, it comes as no surprise that this global 12.7% figure varies hugely between the different regions of the world. In Africa, the figure is just 1.4%, in the Middle East 6.7% and in Asia 7.1%. This compares with 68.3% of the population in North America, 48.5% in Oceania and 31.6% in Europe. However, these figures mask huge variations within each region. In terms of the absolute numbers of internet users, the US still dominates, with well over 202 million users. However, China now comes second. Although the internet penetration rate in China is still low – at just 6.8% – the overall population is of such a size that this figure represents 87 million users. China is followed by Japan with more than 66 million users. The first two European countries – Germany and the United Kingdom – are only fourth and fifth in this global ranking.

Which countries have the highest proportionate rates of internet use? Here a rather different picture emerges. Sweden (where almost three quarters of the adult population are internet users) and Hong Kong (with over 70%) have the highest levels of penetration, with the US only ranking third, with almost 69% of the adult population using the internet. The average level of internet penetration for the top 10 countries is over 66%, which means that the UK – at just 58.5% – still falls outside of the global internet elite.

The focus of this report is on the UK, and we now possess very rich statistical data that make clear that although rates of internet use are continuing to increase (though not so fast as a few years ago), there remain enduring *digital divides* within the population. In 2004, 58% of adults in Great Britain had used the internet in the previous three months[5]. The most common use was for email (85%) and finding information about goods or services (82%). The most frequent place of access was the person's own home (82%), followed by their workplace (42%). At the level of the household, 52% of households in the UK (12.8 million) could access the internet from home, compared with just 9% (2.2 million) in 1998. Twelve per cent of all homes in the UK now have a broadband connection and this figure is increasing fast. Men are still more likely than women to use the internet, but the gap is closing. There is also a marked generational divide in internet usage. It is highest in the 16 to 24 age group (83%) and lowest in the 65 and

---

[4] This figure and the ones that follow derive from www.internetworldstats.com

[5] This figure and the ones that follow for the UK derive from www.statistics.gov.uk – the website of the Office for National Statistics (ONS).

older age group (15%). One of the biggest differences, perhaps not surprisingly, relates to income. In 2003, a full 85% of households in the top income decile had internet access at home, whereas the figure was only 12% for those in the lowest decile – the richest households are over seven times more likely to have internet access than are the poorest.

As we noted earlier, the emergence of the internet has facilitated a huge number of different applications and services, some of which are having a real impact on how we organise our lives. The advent of IBNIS is changing the ways we: search for new neighbourhoods in which to live; decide which school catchment area to live in; decide where to invest in buy-to-let properties; decide what a safe neighbourhood is for our student offspring to reside in; decide whether or not to apply for a particular job in a particular place; and so on. As ever more detailed local knowledge becomes freely available online, people will find myriad ways of using it, the consequences of which have hitherto received little systematic attention (Burrows and Ellison, 2004).

Different types of internet-based neighbourhood information systems

Our focus here is on the emergence of websites that offer:

- *free access*;
- *geographically referenced data of various sorts*; and
- *searchable features*, either in terms of being able to look up information on a particular place (via a postcode, ward, town or city, for example) and/or by being able to locate particular places that conform to some specifiable characteristics (eg www.findyourspot.com).

This working definition of IBNIS means that we are not concerned with websites that simply provide information about particular places (tourism or many local authority websites, for example), unless that information is provided in a manner that is geographically referenced and searchable (eg www.portlandonline.com/oni or www.citystats.org). Neither are we interested in sites that charge a fee for the service of providing bespoke neighbourhood reports (eg www.hometrack.co.uk), although we are interested in those that do this but also provide a more limited service for free (eg www.homecheck.co.uk). Nor are we interested in sites that just offer maps (although such sites are often nested within, or link from, the sites we examine here).

Using this working definition of IBNIS, we have identified at least 33 different websites in the English-speaking world that conform to it as detailed in Figure 2.1. This is not a definitive list as this is an area of socio-technological development that is in a constant state of flux – but the 33 represent a good range of the different types of site available as at the end of 2004.

It is possible to identify four main categories of IBNIS all of which are underpinned by different socioeconomic and political drivers. Most sites can be mapped to one or other of these four types, but some are best considered as hybrids.

- First, there are sites that are explicitly *commercial*. These include sites that offer neighbourhood information in order to attract sponsors and advertising of various sorts interested in place-based marketing services.
- Second, there are those sites that have grown out of the activities of the *geodemographics industry*. These are again commercial sites, but aimed primarily at the marketing industry. These sites are increasingly performing a dual function as geodemographic knowledge becomes something that interests ordinary consumers and internet users as much as it does marketing organisations.
- Third, there are sites aimed at the *policy and research communities* at a national, regional and city level in order to provide data in support of a range of regeneration activities.
- Fourth, there are sites run primarily by charities, political and/or community organisations that utilise the technology in order to provide resources for environmental and/or community development and campaigning purposes. We might term these *social software sites* in order to indicate that they provide IBNIS that aim to contribute from the 'bottom up' towards resources for individuals, groups and communities of various sorts.

Figure 2.1: Internet–based neighbourhood information systems examined

		Url	Type	Detailed summary	Case study
1	ACORN CACI	www.caci.co.uk/acorn	Geodemographic	Yes	No
2	Brighton and Hove City Stats	www.citystats.org	Policy and research (social software)	Yes	No
3	CheckMyFile	www.checkmyfile.com	Commercial (adverts)	Yes	No
4	Chav Towns	www.chavtowns.co.uk	Commercial (purchase + adverts)	No	No
5	Cleveland Neighborhood Link	http://little.nhlink.net/nhlink	Social software	No	No
6	Cleveland's CANDO	http://povertycenter.cwru.edu/	Social software	No	No
7	Chicago Neighborhood Early Warning System	www.cnt.org/news	Social software	No	No
8	Crap Towns	www.craptowns.com	Commercial (purchase)	Yes	No
9	DC Agenda	www.dcagenda.org.nis	Social software	Yes	No
10	East St Louis Geog Info Retrieval System	http://eslarp2.lanarch.uiuc.edu	Social software	No	No
11	Find Your Spot	www.findyourspot.com	Commercial (purchase)	Yes	No
12	Fish 4 Homes	http://fish4.co.uk/homes/ask/areainfo.jsp	Commercial (adverts)	No	No
13	Home Check	www.homecheck.co.uk	Commercial (purchase)	Yes	No
14	Home Store	www.homestore.com	Commercial (adverts)	Yes	No
15	Local Knowledge	www.localknowledge.co.uk	Policy and research (social software)	No	No
16	Minneapolis Neighbourhoods	www.freenet.t.msp.mn.us/nhoods/mpls	Social software	No	No
17	MSN House and Home	http://houseandhome.msn.com	Commercial (geodemographic)	Yes	Yes
18	My Best Segments	www.cluster1.claritas.com/MyBestSegments/Default.jsp	Geodemographic	Yes	No
19	My Florida	www.myflorida.com	Commercial (adverts)	No	No
20	My Village	www.myvillage.com	Commercial (adverts)	No	No
21	Neighborhood Find	www.neighborhoodfind.com	Commercial (adverts)	No	No
22	Neighborhood Knowledge Los Angeles	http://nkla.ucla.edu	Social software	Yes	No
23	Neighbourhood Statistics	http://neighbourhood.statistics.gov.uk	Policy and research	Yes	Yes
24	Office of Neighborhood Involvement Portland	www.myportlandneighborhood.org	Social software (policy and research)	Yes	No
25	Our Property	www.ourproperty.co.uk	Commercial (adverts)	Yes	No
26	Property Value	www.propertyvalue.com.au	Commercial (adverts)	No	No
27	San Diego Geographic Information System	www.sangis.org	Policy and research (social software)	No	No
28	Scorecard	www.scorecard.org	Social software	Yes	Yes
29	Sperling's Best Places (discussed as part of MSN House and Home)	www.bestplaces.net	Commercial (purchase (geodemographic)	No	No
30	UK Villages	www.ukvillages.co.uk	Commercial (adverts)	No	No
31	Up My Street	www.upmystreet.com	Commercial (adverts) (geodemographic) (social software)	Yes	Yes
32	What's In Your Backyard (UK Environment Agency)	http://216.31.193.171/asp/1_introduction.asp?language=English	Policy and research (social software)	Yes	No
33	Yahoo Real Estate	http://Realestate.yahoo.com	Commercial (adverts)	No	No

Website examples

Figure 2.1 lists in alphabetical order the 33 sites that are our primary focus in this report. We provide the URL for each and also attempt to classify each site in terms of typology elucidated above. The figure also notes the subsample of 17 that we examine in more detail below, and the four exemplar sites that we examine in the next chapter.

1 ACORN CACI
www.caci.co.uk/acorn

Geodemographic site example

Provides consumer profiles for marketers and their campaigns but is also available to researchers and the public.

Geography
Postcode.

Type
Commercial. Marketing site for CACI geodemographic products.

ACORN is a leading geodemographic tool in the UK used to identify and understand the UK population and the demand for products and services. Businesses use it to improve their understanding of customers, to target markets and to determine where to locate operations. This site allows members of the public to find out how their neighbourhood is classified. Similar data are also available from CACI via Up My Street.

2 Brighton and Hove City Stats
www.citystats.org

Policy and research site example

Provides detailed maps of crime rates across the area, information on location of services such as GPs and schools, and comparisons of levels of deprivation across the city.

Geography
Ward and 'locally defined communities'.

Type
Policy and research. Some signs of social software.

Data are provided on the basis of variable geographies including 'locally defined communities'. Developments in progress include more detailed reports covering specific areas of interest to local community groups, and also linking to external research carried out by local groups based on the Citystats information. Site is viewed as a strategic tool that can help planning at both local and national level, with information such as the Indices of Deprivation and Census used to allocate funding, and target and evaluate programmes.

3 Check My File
www.checkmyfile.com

Commercial site example

Geography
All freely available data are searchable by postcode and refer to various geographical scales.

Type
Commercial. UK-based. Credit Reporting Agency Limited operates the site, which is aimed at consumers rather than business users. Users have to pay for many of the site's features, but some services are offered with instant access at no charge.

The site provides online information about individuals, their geographical area and their assets. The company claim to be the first, worldwide, to offer consumers the ability to check their own credit score and to give plain English explanations of how credit scoring works. This information, together with information on home area classifications – 'geodemographic data' – is provided free. Users are able to input a postcode to find a range of credit, lifestyle and census information about that area including: details of housing types and the social grades of residents; evaluation of qualification levels and the number of directors in the area; financial information such as the credit risk associated to the postcode and the number of investors in the area; lifestyle information, such as the most common type of newspaper read, the average number of cars per household and gold card ownership levels; a Neighbourhood Environmental Search showing information on flood risk, radon levels, coal mining, landslip, landfill, air quality and pollution; government statistics including age distribution of residents, marital status, ethnic group, religion, health, economic activity and resident population; and links to information on crime rates, house prices, local schools and amenities. Other services provided free to UK consumers include links to help check statutory pension entitlements and to help find the correct address using the Royal Mail Postcode Address File. Users can also use the free credit-scoring service to find suitable credit card lenders. Credit Reporting Agency Ltd claims that both credit score and geodemographic information is often used by lenders when assessing information, but is not included on statutory credit file printouts, and thus would otherwise be inaccessible.

8 Crap Towns
www.craptowns.com

Commercial site example

Laypersons giving their highly individual 'comic' views of places.

Geography
Towns and cities in the UK/Ireland and US.

Type
Commercial. Although there is no advertising as such, the site functions to both generate material for and promote the best-selling Idler *CrapTowns I and CrapTowns II* books.

Descriptions of places can be sent to the authors of the website who then post them. There is no or little statistical data to speak of, just individual supposedly 'comic' opinions. A Java map gives the option to choose between the US and UK/Ireland. After picking the state/nation, one simply follows a link to a city/town. An example posting about Middlesbrough in the North East of England is indicative:

> To begin with it is hard to argue with the state of Middlesbrough town centre. It is indeed a cross between Royston Vasey and a 1920 Pit village. However, Middlesbrough isn't just the town centre. In favour of Middlesbrough is its location. Middlesbrough is a short drive to the North Yorkshire Moors, including the picturesque villages of Castleton, Rosedale and Goathland (where Heartbeat and some scenes from Harry Potter were filmed). Without a doubt the North Yorkshire Moors has some of the country's most beautiful walks and it is this that attracts many people to live in Middlesbrough.

> The intelligent inhabitants of Middlesbrough stay away from the scally's of the Boro and live on the outskirts of Middlesbrough in the plush green suburbs of Nunthorpe, Marton, Ingelby Barwick, Stokesley and Yarm. Here the non-scally residents are shielded from the drug dealers, prostitutes and heroin addicts that frequent the back streets of the Boro. And who can name a town or city that does not suffer drug problems and prostitution?

> Finally, Middlesbrough now has one of the country's best managers helping to guide the Boro in the Premiership. Now that we have rid ourselves of the folly that was Robson, Middlesbrough FC is now seen as a rising star with its manager Steve McClaren strongly tipped as the next England Manager.

> All in all Middlesbrough isn't too bad. There's worse places to live, but I would recommend that you stay out of Middlesbrough at night, and during the day stick to the main streets.

9 DC Agenda's Neighborhood Information Service
www.dcagenda.org/nis

Mission statement: 'Providing community-based organizations and residents in the District with local data and analysis they can use to improve the quality of life in their neighborhoods'. Aimed at community-based organisations and lay people. Started in 1998.

Geography
Clickable maps based on a range of geographies; council wards; Advisory Neighborhood Commissions; Neighborhood Clusters; Police Service Areas; and Census tracts.

Type
Social software.

Using data from sources such as the US Census, Demographic and Housing Data, Vital Statistics Records, Home Mortgage Lending Activity, Subsidized Housing databases, Property Sales, Crime Reports and Arrests, and Child Abuse and Neglect Cases. The site allows statistics and maps to be generated at a number of different levels of granularity. Owned and run by DC Agenda, sponsored by philanthropic support.

11 Find Your Spot
www.findyourspot.com

Website constructed as an online quiz to find the best places to live, work and retire in the US.

Geography
Towns and cities in the US.

Type
Commercial. Although there is no advertising on the site, there is encouragement to register as a member, which, on receipt of a payment, provides access to more detailed reports of particular locations. In order to see results of the quiz, one has to register personal details that can be passed on to various commercial organisations.

A long series of questions about individual preferences, organised in blocks, concerning the weather, culture, teachers, doctors, transport, leisure access, population size and density, dominant socio-demographic characteristics, communities of faith, access to membership of national organisations, local tax levels, housing costs and so on. It is not clear which databases underpin the 'quiz' but most appear to be in the public domain. It is possible to restrict the search to particular regions of the US. It is claimed that 1.1 million people complete the quiz each year. A privately held company based in Colorado led by Brent Eskew, an attorney and real estate broker, runs the site. The site was launched in 1997. On completing the quiz, the first named author was informed by the site that his 'best spot' was in Boston, Massachusetts.

13 Home Check – "Don't buy a home without us"
www.homecheck.co.uk

Provides postcode-level data on property and environmental risks and some basic socio-demographic neighbourhood data to members of the public.

Geography
Postcode.

Type
Commercial. UK-based. Small amounts of advertising, but basic 'free' home-check service acts as a conduit to an information service for lawyers, banks, surveyors, insurance companies, engineers and other property professionals

via www.homecheckpro.co.uk. The site is likely to become more commercial as it develops a more detailed online data service in anticipation of the launch of compulsory home sellers' packs.

Popular website managed by Sitescope information using data taken from a number of agencies. Information concentrates on flood statistics and air quality data taken from the Environmental Agency and AEA Technology. Clear map-based information done in partnership with Francis Fifth Collection providing access to historical Ordnance Survey maps. Service developed in partnership with the many organisations. Homecheck Area Reports provide data on local authority information, crime statistics, education, amenities, people and the housing market. Postcoded environmental risk reports are central to the site. Home Check is managed centrally by Sitescope Ltd, whose services are based on one of the largest property and environmental risk databases in Europe. Information is supplied under licence from Ordnance Survey, the Environment Agency, the British Geological Survey, the Valuation Office, English Nature and the Office of the Deputy Prime Minister. Sitescope Ltd was acquired by DMG Information Ltd, the parent company of Landmark Information Group, in July 2003. The intended audience is both private homebuyers and professionals linked to the property market. The site was launched in June 2003.

14 Home Store
www.homestore.com

Commercial site example

The Home Store network provides web-based information with home- and real estate-related content, including a number of tools allowing users to locate neighbourhoods, towns and cities with certain characteristics.

Geography
Zip codes, towns, cities and states.

Type
Commercial. US-based site full of advertising and links to commercial organisations involved in real estate, housing finance and relocations. Closely tied in with the realtor industry, especially www.realtor.com.

Site allows users to use various 'neighbourhood search tools'. City Comparison allows any two cities to be compared in relation to demography, climate, cost of living, education, major employers and so on. Neighbourhood Finder allows users to match zip codes with similar geodemographic characteristics across states and cities and/or specify some limited socioeconomic and house price criteria in order to locate zip codes that match these preferences. City Matchmaker functions rather like www.findyourspot.com – although it is rather less sophisticated – in order to find towns and cities that match a limited set of preferences. The data that underpin these tools are collected by Home Store research staff from various official and commercial sources. The site has close links with: www.realtor.com, the official site of the National Association of Realtors; www.homebuilder.com, the official new homes site of the National Association of Home Builders; www.rwentnet.com, an apartments, senior housing, corporate housing and self-storage resource; and HomeStore, a home-related information site with a mortgage financing emphasis. The current site is the product of bringing together these various different sites over the past few years, the earliest of which launched in 1999.

17 MSN House and Home
www.houseandhome.msn.com

Geodemographic site example

Neighbourhood finder for people looking for somewhere to move.

Geography
Zip codes, towns, cities and states.

Type
Commercial. US-based site full of advertising and links to commercial organisations involved in real estate, housing finance and relocations. Also some links to the geodemographics industry.

State-of-the-art neighbourhood finder and comparison portal. It links to various data sources including Claritas' PRIZM segmentation – a geodemographic system covering all US zip codes – and the Portland-based Sperling's Best Places – www.bestplaces.net – database, which, since 1985, draws on demographic and other information to show the 'best places' to work, live and retire in the US. Users can input their preferences and a list of zip codes, towns or cities can be produced. Various comparisons between places can also be made. Launched originally in 1998. *For more information, see case study in Chapter 3.*

18 My Best Segments – "consumer segments defined and described" You are Where you Live
www.cluster1.claritas.com/MyBestSegments/Default.jsp

Geodemographic site example

Provides consumer profiles for marketers and their campaigns but is also available to researchers and the public.

Geography
Zip code.

Type
Commercial. Marketing site for Claritas Inc geodemographic products. Data also available via MSN House and Home and some other sites.

Geodemographic website that allows people to examine how a particular zip code is characterised using a number of different classification systems all owned by Claritas' PRIZM (64 segments); Microvision Standard – 11 groups with 50 segments examining daytime occupation patterns; LifeP$YCLE – 12 household types with distinct usage patterns for insurance products and services; P$YCLE (42 segments); ConneXions – 10 household groups and 60 segments geared towards sellers of communication products and services; and PRIZM New Edition (67 segments). The site provides data on the likelihood of households in a zip code area belonging to certain segment category. Claritas Inc is based in San Diego, California. Data provided online since 1996. The company has been involved in geodemographics since Jonathan Robbin founded it in 1961.

22 Neighborhood Knowledge Los Angeles
http://nkla.ucla.edu

Social software site example

Provision of neighbourhood and housing data that helps predict neighbourhood disinvestments so that community organisations and residents can efficiently target areas for intervention.

Geography
Zip codes in Los Angeles.

Type
Political and campaigning.

Geodemographic data, property data and living quality data available at zip code, Census tract and council levels in both English and Spanish. Developed and maintained by UCLA Advanced Policy Institute in collaboration with various community groups. Founded in 1996, but appears currently not to have been maintained since some time in 2003. Makes available to the public otherwise difficult to access databases. A detailed analysis of this site and comparisons with similar initiatives in other US cities can be found in Krouk et al (2000).

23 Neighbourhood Statistics
neighbourhood.statistics.gov.uk

Part of National Statistics Online. Internet-based government information service that aims to supply information for the National Strategy for Neighbourhood Renewal.

Geography
National, regional, county, local authority, ward, Super Output Area and Output Area level data accessed via postcodes and clickable map that can focus on individual streets and houses.

Type
Policy and research data source, although there is some evidence that it is also being used by members of the public.

Site managed by the Office for National Statistics (ONS), together with a joint initiative involving both central and local government. It provides access to a range of social and economic data relating to small-area geography. Use of Geographic Information Systems to give precise point references for the location of local services and amenities. Use of a UK map where users can click on the region they are interested in, enter a postcode or select a region from a drop-down menu. From there the user gets taken to a further map of your region. This allows users to either select local authority data or dig down even further, right down to ward level and first-point-referenced data. The service developed in partnership with the many organisations that collect data that inform the National Strategy for Neighbourhood Renewal. It is clearly indicated that this is a government-run site. Launched in February 2001. The service will be developed allowing for detailed neighbourhood analysis down to first-point-referenced data (location of services and social/physical infrastructure). *For more information, see case study in Chapter 3.*

24 Office of Neighborhood Involvement Portland
www.myportlandneighborhood.org

Neighbourhood and local information for city of Portland, Oregon.

Geography
Zip code, street name, address.

Type
Social software.

State-of-the-art city-based resource produced by the Office of Neighborhood Involvement (ONI), a city bureau, funded by general fund dollars. Established in 1974, ONI works in partnership with neighbourhoods, business and the Portland State University. Largely based on census information, including 2000 Census for Portland Neighborhoods, General 2000 Census Data, 1996 American Community Survey, 1990 Census Data for Portland Neighborhoods and bureaucratic statistics. Data are collated in cooperation with corporate GIS companies. Maps are produced in partnership with the individual neighbourhood association, District Neighborhood Coalitions and Offices, Portland Bureau of Planning, Portland Office of Transportation, Metro, Multnomah County Assessment and Taxation and Oregon Department of Revenue. It is possible to carry out online graphical profiling including map-based data showing schools, sewerage provision, pollutants, property, crime (further subdivided), neighbourhoods, parks, water utilities, hazards, paving moratorium, elevation, zoning, urban renewal areas, aerial photos, and capital projects. There are also hot links to census data providing information on population projections, income, poverty, housing and genealogy. The online 'crime mapper' (www.gis.ci.portland.or.us/maps/police) is indicative of what the system can offer, allowing detailed street-by-street mapping of a range of different crimes.

25 Our Property
www.ourproperty.co.uk

Geography
All freely available data are searchable by postcode.

Type
Commercial (but with social software rhetoric).

Launched in February 2005, www.ourproperty.co.uk enables users to find out the actual sales price paid for residential property in England and Wales, for every transaction since April 2000 and includes information not only on price paid, but also the full address, the completion date and the property type, such as 'detached'. The dataset is a version of the dataset supplied by HM Land Registry, which, according to the site, is updated monthly and is usually two months behind the property sales. After registration, the site allows members of the public 20 free searches per week, although users can 'top up' their allocation by an additional five searches, either by recommending a friend or subscribing to the newsletter. A simple search involves the user typing in a postcode in a box on the home page. The site then takes the user to a results page, which shows, in the first instance, the amount of sales that have taken place in that area over the past two years and the average price according to property type. Users can then modify the search criteria to search for full 'postcode, road, area or town', or change the time period of search from the default of two years to 'all years' or a specific year from 2000 to 2004. Scroll down the page and information on 'roads in or near your area' is displayed. Within each road/street is the number of sales, average price and a www.multimap.com link to show the location. Clicking on the road denotes a search and information about specific houses is shown. Users are also able to conduct an advanced search, which allows them to input a particular street, town/city, postcode, and/or choose to search by house type (for example, detached) and/or tenure (for example, freehold). Within the advanced search, users can also select a date range. Fubra, the UK internet consultancy that developed the site, claims in part to have done so to offer a social service. The site nonetheless also acts as a showpiece to demonstrate what the company can do for its actual and potential clients. There is certainly interest in such a service. In the first two weeks of its launch, the site received over 150,000 visits and has created a fair amount of media attention.

28 Score Card
www.scorecard.org

Zip code search-based website identifying what pollutants are being released into particular communities and who is responsible.

Geography
Zip codes.

Type
Political and campaigning. Aimed at general public and researchers to identify environmental issues as well as possible solutions.

Score Card ranks and compares the pollution situation in areas across the US, encouraging and enabling users to take action by contacting elected representatives, or volunteering with environmental organisations working in their community. Over 400 scientific and governmental databases are integrated to generate customised profiles of local environmental quality and toxic chemicals. Currently, Score Card's main source of data is derived from the Environmental Protection Agency, including air, water, land, waste, environmental policy and chemical information. Financially supported by the Clarence E. Heller Charitable Foundation of San Francisco, the Joyce Foundation of Chicago, and the New York Community Trust, and by contributions from the members of the Environmental Defence. The site also has support from Oracle Corporation and Environmental Systems Research Institute. Also contains discussion forums on pollution for a specific county area, or in relation to a particular company. Users can also conduct a full text search of the site's bulletin boards. Launched in April 1998. *For more information, see case study in Chapter 3.*

31 Up My Street – "the real-life guide to your neighbourhood"   `Commercial site example`
www.upmystreet.com

Information aimed at lay people on various aspects of their local environment (access to public transport, political representation, neighbourhood profiles and so on).

Geography
All data organised by postcodes, but data refer to various geographic scales, including postcodes, wards, local authorities, political constituencies and so on.

Type
Commercial. UK-based. The site contains much advertising and many commercial and public service links. However, there is also a strong rhetorical ethos of the site being part of the 'social software' genre – a resource for building local social capital. Also some links to the geodemographics industry.

The site provides a useful integration of very different forms of data organised by postcode. There are statistical data provided by a number of agencies – government departments, local authorities and private companies to which Up My Street is licence holder. There are geodemographic data (in the form of ACORN) provided by CACI Ltd. There is a 'conversations' section in which lay people provide information from 'the gound' in response to questions about local issues. There are links to maps via www.multimap.com. Set up in September 1998 and bought by www.uswitch.com on 14 May 2003. *For more information, see case study in Chapter 3.*

32 What's in Your Backyard (UK Environment Agency)   `Commercial site example`
http://216.31.193.171/asp/1_introduction.asp?language=English

Geography
Postcode.

Type
Policy, research, political.

What's in Your Backyard provides online access to the Environment Agency's environmental data for England and Wales. The datasets available provide information on the quality of bathing waters, what substances are being released into the sea, floodplains and flood warnings, the location of landfill sites, what pollution is being emitted from industrial sites, river quality and urban waste water treatment (sewage). The data available on the site are extensive. Examples include the Bathing Waters Directive database, which contains details on 493 coastal and nine inland bathing waters within England and Wales and details analysis on total coliforms, faecal coliforms, faecal streptococci, mineral oils, surface active agents, phenols, pH, salmonellae and enterovirus. Discharges to the Sea details measurements at over 300 coastal sites on substances such as mercury, cadmium, copper, zinc, lead, PCB, gamma-HCH, orthophosphate, nitrogen (total), and Suspended Particulate Material. The Pollution Inventory contains details of 170 chemical substances emitted to air, rivers, estuaries, the sea and sewers from large industrial sites regulated by the Environment Agency in the following sectors: fuel and power production, metal production and processing, mineral industries, chemical industries, waste disposal and recycling, other industries (these include paper, pulp and board manufacturing, and tar and bitumen activities), sewage treatment works, and sites authorised to use radioactive materials. Users can search the data in two ways: through data search or data maps. When using data search, users have to choose a dataset and they are then given various options through which to search the data. In all cases apart from Discharges to the Sea, users are able to search via postcode. When searching by postcode, the user can enter either a full or partial postcode and can then search within a 10-mile, five-mile or one-mile radius from that postcode site. In addition to postcodes, other search options include: operator's name, license number, authority, grid reference, beach, coastal zone, discharge source, place name or company. A postcode search will provide the user with a list of pollution sites, upon which the user can then click to obtain a detailed analysis of pollution releases. Users can also search all the data for any area on the sites data maps by using a postcode, a place name or a grid reference. Once a postcode is entered, the user is able to zoom in or out to view where the pollution sites are located.

Geodemographics

It is clear from Figure 2.1 that the geodemographics industry is important because it supplies data to a range of commercial websites and also directly to the public. Although readers may be familiar with the other main stakeholders in these different forms of IBNIS – commerce, central and local government, community and campaigning groups and so on – they might not be so familiar with the operations of the geodemographics industry and the marketing classifications that the industry produces and promulgates.

The person conventionally credited with the 'invention' of geodemographics is Jonathan Robbin (Goss, 1995b, p 133; Weiss, 2000, p 24). Robbin worked in the Department of Sociology at New York University in the 1950s and 1960s. During this time, he contributed to the development of some of the first computer software for large-scale multivariate statistical analysis – crucially, systems to carry out factor and cluster analysis. In 1961, he left the academy to become an entrepreneur by applying his sociological and statistical insights to a number of social and business problems. In the early 1970s, he "combined the theories of the Chicago school, particularly the notion of ecological competition for urban space between social groups, with the ... factorial ecologies of positivist urban social sciences, to produce ... profiles of residential ZIP code areas" (Goss, 1995a, pp 133-4). Much of the background work to what was to become the first geodemographic system – PRIZM (Potential Rating Index for ZIP Markets) – was grounded not in the world of commerce but in urban policy. The US Department of Housing and Urban Development funded Robbin to develop a system for targeting housing grants to cities with a history of rioting (Weiss, 2000, p 142) and out of this work grew PRIZM. PRIZM was based on a cluster analysis of aggregate data derived both from the US Census and individual data from consumer surveys. PRIZM is now owned and marketed by Claritas and has, over the years, been through numerous iterations.

At the same time as Robbin was developing PRIZM in the US, a social scientist in the UK, Richard Webber, was developing similar ideas. While at the Centre for Environmental Studies in the 1970s, Webber undertook work in Liverpool, the primary intention of which was to provide a better understanding of patterns of urban deprivation in that city. This work led to the development of a software package specifically designed to help government identify clusters of neighbourhoods for which different types of urban deprivation interventions were appropriate (Webber and Craig, 1976, 1978).

Out of this work grew the first UK-based geodemographic classification – ACORN (A Classification of Residential Neighbourhoods). Like Robbin, Webber left the domain of academia and urban policy to develop his system in more commercial directions. He moved to CACI in order to market ACORN and this system became widely used in both public and private sector applications as a means of profiling customers based on their postcodes. In 1985, Webber left CACI to join Experian (which was called CCN at that time) – a company that advertises itself as the leading credit reference agency in the UK – where he developed a new system known as MOSAIC. The MOSAIC classification, released from 1986 onwards, drew upon ancillary datasets to which Experian had access as a result of its credit referencing activities, including electoral data, credit applications and county court judgements by postcode. Webber (2004, p 220) himself observes that it "is ironic that a tool originally designed to distinguish between different categories of poor areas came to be used as a tool for differentiating between different categories of rich people".

The original premise of geodemographic classification was the observation that "people tend to live with others like themselves, sharing similar demographics, lifestyles and values" (Weiss, 2000, p 305). This cluster model is based upon what Claritas, the owners of PRIZM in the US, calls "the fundamental sociological truism that 'birds of a feather flock together' ... or that 'you are where you live'" (quoted in Goss, 1995b, p 134). Certainly, it is the case that, from the point of view of marketing professionals, knowledge of where someone lives is a particularly powerful predictor of all manner of consumption practices, values, tastes, preferences and so on.

The specific ways in which these classifications are compiled vary among different software developers, but most share a common methodological approach. This is not the place to detail the statistical intricacies involved, but the basic idea is straightforward enough. A large number of geographically referenced data items – about half from the Census and the other half from other (mostly commercial) sources – are subject to a form of statistical cluster analysis (although often manual interventions also occur in order to 'correct' for any obvious anomalies that might be generated). The resulting classification is then subject to various evaluations that can lead to changes. The resulting classification is then 'trained' by seeing how well it predicts geographical variations in consumption and 'lifestyle' variables derived from surveys not included in the process of producing the initial version of the classification. The weighting of the variables is then recalibrated in order to produce a classification that gives the greatest level of discrimination when predicting differences in consumption patterns between different types of place. Finally, some manual interventions or 'judgements' might occur – such as deciding to merge two fairly similar clusters and/or differentiating between urban/rural places that otherwise appear very similar. The final (and perhaps most difficult) task is then to 'label' each type of place in a manner that epitomises its dominant characteristics. This done, the combination of variables that have been fused together to form each category of place is then carefully characterised via the production of a detailed 'qualitative' narrative aimed at producing a sense of the 'sort of people' who reside within neighbourhoods so classified.

By way of illustration, Appendix A shows the current ACORN and MOSAIC classifications for the UK. Both are based on the UK postcode geography. There are currently some 1.7 million postcodes in the UK, each on average covering about 14 houses. Each of these postcodes can be allocated to a particular ACORN category, group or type or a particular MOSAIC group or type. Both ACORN and MOSAIC provide highly detailed characterisations of all of these types of neighbourhood. We have seen a brief example of this in our opening chapter from the Up My Street website, where we saw how the ACORN type *older professionals in detached houses and apartments type* was characterised.

By way of a further illustration, MOSAIC classifies the postcode where the first named author currently resides as *town and gown transition*, which it summarises as follows: 'Students and academics mix with young professionals in terraces relatively close to universities'. The names 'Tom' and 'Kate' are apparently popular in such neighbourhoods. The 'key features' of such neighbourhoods are given as: singles; mature students; postgraduates; idealistic and headstrong; freedom from careerdom; low incomes; alternative lifestyles; liberal-minded; and socialising with friends. Twelve dense pages of text, photos, graphs and charts summarise the 'ideal typical' character of such places under the headings of: sociology and environment; culture and consumer psychology; stereotype; who we are; how we make a living; where we live; our home lives; *Weltanschauung*; time use; and measures of deprivation. Space precludes a detailed summary of this material but people living in such places are significantly more likely than average to like: art; books; film; computer games; cycling; fashion; going to the pub; hiking and walking; using the internet; pop and rock music; theatre; and wine. They are also significantly more likely than the average to read the *Economist, Guardian, Independent, Observer, Times* and *New Statesman*.

Affluent blue-collar neighbourhoods, on the other hand, the ACORN type that covers the postcode of the first named author's parents' bungalow, are summarised as: 'Older manual workers with a good standard of living in comfortable semis where traditional working class values are held'. The names 'Barrie' and 'Marlene' are suggested as emblematic. The 'key features' of such neighbourhoods are given as: older manual workers; steady employment; secure family life; high standard of living; spacious semis; safe areas; traditional; TV, pubs, eating out; and no interest in the internet. People living in such places are significantly more likely than average to like: caravanning; eating out; feeding garden birds; watching football; gardening; grandchildren; and motoring. They are also significantly more likely than the average to read the *Daily Mail, Express, Mirror* and *People*.

MOSAIC alone is used by over 10,000 different organisations for purposes of direct marketing and such classifications are also increasingly used in policy and research contexts as they have been found to provide more subtle accounts of neighbourhood variation than is possible using other variables.

None of this is news. Such classifications have
been a major feature of commercial and public
sector activities for some time now and their
impact has been the subject of much academic
comment and research effort (Goss, 1995a,
1995b; Pickles, 1995; Harris and Weiner, 1996;
Curry, 1998; Graham and Marvin, 2001, pp 239-
42; Janes and Mooney, 2002; Lyon, 2002a, 2000b;
Monmonier, 2002; Phillips and Curry, 2002;
Elmer, 2004; Graham, 2004). What is of interest to
us in this report is the possibility that such
geodemographic classifications are beginning to
migrate from the software of marketing and
policy research organisations into the public
domain, via IBNIS, as a way of characterising
places. How marketing and policy organisations
characterise particular streets could be becoming
just as much a part of local knowledge as the
report of the local school from the Office for
Standards in Education, the distance to the
nearest flood plain or the average price of local
houses.

Four case studies

In this chapter, we examine four exemplar case studies of internet-based neighbourhood information systems (IBNIS): Up My Street in the UK and MSN House and Home in the US are both leading examples of commercial sites with strong links to the geodemographics industry; Neighbourhood Statistics run by the Office for National Statistics in the UK is a state-of-the-art site for policy and research; and Score Card is a leading US example of how IBNIS can be used as a form of social software for political campaigning purposes – in this instance environmental politics.

1 Up My Street (www.upmystreet.com)

Up My Street (UMS) is a 'front-line' commercial website that claims to be the "UK's leading provider of local information". The website is designed to help people find out more about particular neighbourhoods and allows comparisons to be made between neighbourhoods. Users enter their postcode or town on the site to access relevant information about that geographical area. Information is grouped under the following search categories:

- **property**, which provides a guide to local property prices and makes comparisons with the national average; searches for estate agents; checks council tax rates; compares mortgages; and locates local solicitors or conveyance firms;
- **FindMyNearest...**™, a local business directory;
- **classifieds**, a service to advertise houses, cars and so on;
- **conversations**, a message board to promote user discussions about their local areas;

- **education**, which provides figures on local school performance and compares them against the national average;
- **policing and crime**, which provides crime statistics and compares them against the national average;
- **ACORN profile**, which aims to illustrate likely consumer preferences and behaviour;
- **people**, which gives statistics on population, average weekly pay and unemployment and compares them with the national average;
- **weather**, which gives a local forecast;
- **public transport**, which gives the user distances from their postcode to nearest train and bus stations, airports and so on;
- **council performance**, which provides performance indicators on the local council;
- **contacting your council** and **your representative**, which provide contact details for the local council, councillors, the local MP and the MEPs.

Aztec Internet, a digital media consultancy, launched www.upmystreet.com in September 1998, initially as a 'marketing demonstration site' designed to display Aztec's technical skills and knowledge with database and information management (Butcher, 2003; Witchells, 2003). The original advocates of UMS at Aztec were Tom Loosemore (content strategist) and Stefan Magdalinski (chief technology officer). Tony Blin-Stoyle, another key figure in the site's history, joined as managing director in 2000. Loosemore was particularly influential in developing user interaction systems and was the originator of UMS Conversations (eventually launched in October 2002), which was one of the first projects to map the comments of residents to places. In 2003, Loosemore headed up BBCi Connect, which oversees the interaction of the

BBC's viewers and listeners via message boards and chat rooms.

As a limited company, in 1999 UMS went into partnership with Open Interactive, the pre-Sky Interactive TV business. After News International invested £9 million in 2000, UMS joined with the investment bank N.M. Rothschild, which invested a further £12 million (Gibson, 2003a, 2003b). In 2000, UMS also entered into collaboration with market analyst company, CACI Ltd, to form one of the first online consumer geodemographic profiling services at postcode level.

In 2001, UMS participated in the Office of the Deputy Prime Minister's Pathfinder scheme and entered into a multi-agency partnership to establish SomersetOnLine, which aimed "to deliver unified services to the people of Somerset, via the SomersetOnLine Portal web site and Digital TV" (DigiTV, 2004). Some of the principal objectives of SomersetOnLine were to provide a simple means of fault reporting, form requests, requesting a housing repair, reporting a stolen/dumped car, locating local home help services, participating in public consultations, contacting a councillor and applying for jobs. In addition, other objectives included using the system to widen the participation and inclusion of people accessing public services within Somerset and to "provide joined-up local government in Somerset".

Valued at £43 million in 2000 during the height of the dot.com boom, by 2002 UMS struck financial difficulties and managing director Tony Blin-Stoyle made a number of redundancies in an effort to move the company towards a break-even point, but in April 2003 the company went into administration. UMS brought in accountants RSM Robson Rhodes to seek an administration order and attempt to attract new investment. Eventually, Uswitch.com (a website that compares prices of utilities such as gas and water) bought the company, but both Blin-Stoyle and Stefan Magdalinski left the company (Gibson, 2003a, 2003b; Witchells, 2003).

In 2003, around half of UMS's revenue came from advertising and sponsorship with the other half generated from consultation and syndicating the website's content (Online Publishing News, 2002; Witchells, 2003). Through FindMyNearest...™, UMS offers a means by which companies can advertise in particular local areas, and in

partnership with *Exchange & Mart* and *AdTrader*, the company also offers advertising through its classifieds service. Sponsorship is a method by which UMS can place a company name or a brand logo at key points within the website. For example, Gleeson Homes supplied UMS with information on the geographical areas on which it intended to develop. UMS then identified the postcodes of those areas and placed a message from Gleeson Homes on the relevant pages. Similarly, UMS will place text boxes, links and/or logos of companies in relevant areas on their site, so, for example, Which? has a place at the base of the property prices block, with a message to encourage home movers and those planning to move to click on the text link or logo to see how Which? Online could help their home move.

Syndicating the website's content basically involves UMS providing a number of ways in which it can 'enhance' company websites by adding the means to access local information in a similar manner to UMS (www.upmystreet.com). Currently, the company's private sector clients include: Bryant Homes, Connells, Hamptons, nPower, Powergen, Royal Bank of Scotland, Sequence, Which?, HSBC, Halifax, AOL and Thompson Directories.

A future project currently under consideration is for UMS to produce an index that would give overall scores to particular postcodes and thus provide another means of comparison between geographical areas.

2 MSN House and Home/Sperling's Best Places (www.houseandhome.msn.com)

MSN House and Home originated in 1998 as www.homeadvisor.com under the leadership of Ian Morris, the then Project Unit Manager of HomeAdvisor Technologies. Microsoft renamed the site www.houseandhome.msn.com in late 2002 as part of the corporation's launch of its new ISP services, MSN 8. House and Home quickly became one of the most aggressive and best-funded real estate/e-commerce websites in the US, with financial backing coming not only from Microsoft, but also other large investors, including chase.com and Norwest Mortgage. Until 2004, House and Home had two principal competitors, realtor.com and homestore.com, but partnership deals with both these former rivals meant that each now provides advertising, listing and information at MSN's House and Home site.

Through www.realtor.com, www.homebuilder.com and www.realtytrac.com, House and Home enables potential property buyers to search for previously owned, new or foreclosed properties across both the US and Canada. Site users can perform searches by city, state, zip code and/or price range. Users can also search for rented properties in the same way, with the information provided by rentnet.com.

House and Home also has sections that it targets to buyers/renters who do not yet have specific geographical areas in mind. 'Find a neighbourhood' and 'Find the best city for me' facilitate searches and comparisons of geographical locations across the US. Using Sperling's bestplaces.net, which includes data on 3,000 city profiles, statistics on 87,000 schools and crime rates in 2,500 cities, users are able to select from a range of criteria to search for cities and/or neighbourhoods. Searching by region, city or state, users can find neighbourhoods that match the ones they currently live in, and/or call up a set of criteria to compare geographical areas, including:

- population
- school rating
- cost-of-living index
- average home price
- income tax rate
- future job growth
- number of sunny days
- air quality
- water quality
- violent crime

On the 'Find the best city for me' facility, users encounter a table that makes direct city comparisons with statistics displayed on:

- demographics
- cost-of-living index
- schools
- degree holders
- crime
- housing
- economy
- health
- climate

The table also includes a comparison of both cities against the national average, with values that are worse than the national average showing up in red. Included in these sections of the site are also cost-of-living and salary calculator tools that allow users to compare how far their salary will go in different geographical locations.

Once users have presumably settled on the place they want to live and found the home they want, House and Home directs them to areas of the site where they can check their credit ratings via Experian, and then arrange mortgages, loans, insurance and so on through MSN's finance partners.

3 Neighbourhood Statistics (www.neighbourhood.statistics.gov.uk)

The Office for National Statistics (ONS) launched the Neighbourhood Statistics service in February 2001 in response to recommendations from the report of Policy Action Team (PAT) 18, *Better information*, in April 2000 (PAT 18, 2000). The ONS established PAT 18 to address some of the problems identified in the Social Exclusion Unit's (SEU) 1998 report, *Bringing Britain together: A national strategy for neighbourhood renewal* (SEU, 1998). One of the problems highlighted by the SEU report were the difficulties involved in the accumulation and assembling of disparate and often incompatible forms of data about the deprived neighbourhoods under investigation. In short, although it was apparent that much of the data existed, it was also evident that government had "never set out to record or analyse" this data in a "comprehensive or systematic way" (PAT 18, 2000, p 7). PAT 18 thus considered that there was "a strong case for central government to take the lead in drawing together a range of data about neighbourhoods" and that this "might be termed Neighbourhood Statistics" (PAT 18, 2000, p 24).

It was not the intention of PAT 18 that Neighbourhood Statistics should define a set of performance measures or management targets. Instead, PAT 18 considered that Neighbourhood Statistics would enable and empower organisations such as the National Strategy for Neighbourhood Renewal (NSNR), local people and neighbourhood managers, by "ensuring the presence of a better infrastructure and the availability of better data that would allow them to focus on small areas across a wide range of issues" (PAT 18, 2000, p 27).

The delivery of Neighbourhood Statistics was also part of a wider e-Business strategy within the ONS of which the main objective is to develop the 'internet as a public source of statistical information'. Strong support for the PAT 18 recommendations came from both within the ONS and from other interested parties, such as the NSNR and the Statistics Commission. The repeated criticism that statistical data were both difficult to locate and often inadequate for the identification and targeting of local problems created a context within which there was uniform support for the proposal that the ONS should provide a 'one-stop shop' for Neighbourhood Statistics (Statistics Commission, 2001; ONS, 2002).

The Statistics Commission considered that Neighbourhood Statistics would have "very wide value" that would likely go "far beyond the needs of central government". Indeed, other than both national and local government, the ONS envisages a wide range of users, including health authorities, police and fire authorities, professionals and commentators, businesses and citizens (ONS, 2004b).

Although the ONS manages Neighbourhood Statistics centrally, other government and non-government organisations supplement and support the programme through the supply of data, planning and review (ONS, 2004a). These include:

- Department for Constitutional Affairs
- Department for Culture, Media and Sport
- Department for Education and Skills
- Department for Environment, Food and Rural Affairs
- Department of Trade and Industry
- Department of Transport
- Department for Work and Pensions
- Department of Health
- Her Majesty's Treasury
- Home Office
- Inland Revenue
- Local Government Association
- Office of the Deputy Prime Minister
- Ordnance Survey
- Social Exclusion Unit

The ONS developed Neighbourhood Statistics through three distinct stages. Stage 1 involved the release of 15 datasets at ward level onto a prototype system. During stage 2, the ONS incorporated a geographical information system within Neighbourhood Statistics, which provides background Ordnance Survey maps to show the geographical areas covered. With the implementation of stage 2, users were able to search for data by place name and postcode. Stage 2 also included an intermediate phase to enable the ONS to release the first wave of Census 2001 statistics. A redesign of the website during this phase also included the addition of three new ways that users could search for statistics:

(i) by subject (such as crime or housing etc);
(ii) by area name (such as London or North East etc);
(iii) through an interactive map, which allows users to 'drill down' through the map to their area of interest.

In stage 3, the ONS released Census 2001 statistics for small geographical areas, with key statistics available for 8,850 wards and 175,000 'output areas'. The ONS developed the use of output areas to overcome problems associated with the varying size of electoral wards across the country and frequent boundary changes. In line with Census 2001, an output area consists of 125 households and 300 people per unit. However, because of some disclosure and confidentiality problems, the ONS will develop 'super output areas' for some datasets, which will come in three layers of 1,000, 5,000 and 20,000 people respectively (ONS, 2004a).

Since February 2003, any member of the public has been able to use Neighbourhood Statistics to access census and other statistical data online free of charge; use a geographical information system to show areas covered by wards; search by place name and/or postcode; and select areas and generate, arrange and manipulate tables online for cross-boundary analysis. By January 2005, the ONS intends England to have a web-based statistical system for small geographic areas that will disseminate information on the following (ONS, 2004a):

Access to services
- access to cars and vans
- travel to work
- education services
- health services

Community well-being
- caring responsibilities
- population turnover
- satisfaction with local government services
- social capital

Community safety
- notification offences recorded by the police
- domestic burglary incidents
- victimisation
- fires

Economic deprivation
- Family Credit claimants
- Income Support claimants
- Housing Benefit/Council Tax Benefit claimants
- distribution of household incomes

Education, skills and training
- university admissions by place of residence
- primary school pupils at key stage 2
- qualifications
- students

Health
- Attendance Allowance claimants
- Disability Living Allowance claimants
- hospital episode statistics
- limiting long-standing illness
- good/not good health
- dental caries in children
- children in need
- life expectancy
- premature or avoidable mortality

Housing
- changes of ownership by price
- dwelling stock by council tax band
- tenure
- household facilities
- vacant and second homes
- poor quality housing fitness, cost of repairs and so on
- vacant stock by council tax band
- housing association rents and incomes for dwellings let

Physical environment
- vacant commercial and industrial space

Work deprivation
- Jobseeker's Allowance claimants
- Incapacity Benefit claimants
- Severe Disablement Allowance claimants
- VAT registered enterprises by industry
- VAT registered enterprises by employment size
- employee jobs
- claimant count
- employment status by occupation

People and society
- population by age/sex/ethnic group
- household size and structure
- population estimates for wards, mid-1998
- vital statistics, 1998
- population estimates for local authorities, mid-1998
- Parliamentary Electorate, 1997-98 (England); 1994-98 (Wales)

4 Score Card (www.scorecard.org)

Score Card is a political as opposed to a commercial website concerned with the public disclosure of pollution and toxic chemicals in the US. Drawing on data generated from over 400 scientific and governmental database sources, such as the US Environmental Protection Agency's Toxic Release Inventory (TRI), National Emissions Trend and Air Quality System databases, and the Clean Water Act, Score Card provides a localised environmental map with the aim of exposing which geographic areas and companies have the worst pollution records.

Environmental Defense launched Score Card on 22 April 1998 (Earth Day) when the site received more than one million hits in 24 hours, which at that time was a record for any non-profit website. Originating with Bill Pease, Score Card arose as a solution to the logistical problems of information disclosure on pollution across different geographical areas. Pease, who joined Environmental Defense in 1995, was part of a team that secured funding to provide services to community-based environmental organisations that required technical assistance in assessing different types of polluting behaviour in their neighbourhood. It soon became apparent to Pease that many of these groups were asking for similar kinds of information and that he was regularly going to the same sources to answer their questions. Thus, Pease began to think about ways in which Environmental Defense could provide an information technology-based system that would make information on pollution available to communities across the US in an accessible format.

However, while Pease and his team knew what kind of information they wanted to make available, they did not know how to make it widely available. To realise his idea, Pease entered into collaboration with Philip Greenspun, who at that time was a graduate student at the Massachusetts Institute of Technology, but more importantly was also involved in building open access web-based services. Greenspun convinced Pease to adopt a web browser-based system and, in 1996, Pease persuaded both Environmental Defense and the Clarence E. Heller Charitable Foundation of San Francisco to fund the web-based project. Data modelling and collection began in late 1996 and Pease and Greenspun started the programming in mid-1997, which they completed in early 1998 ready for the website's launch in April of that year.

Fred Krupp, Executive Director of Environmental Defense, describes the goal of Score Card as making "the local environment as easy to check on as the local weather" (Krupp, 2004). The initial intent was to solve the problem outlined above – to provide important scientific and technical information to community-based environmental organisations and thus empower community organisers towards successful anti-pollution campaigns. Environmental Defense thus saw Score Card as a tool to stigmatise the poor environmental performance of top US polluters and to generate online lobbying, thereby increasing constituency pressure on legislative debates about the environment. As Benjamin Smith, Environmental Defense outreach coordinator, recalled, the idea was "to give people information and documentation and the kinds of tools they need to take action" (Price, 2000, p 10). In this regard, Pease worked closely with David Roe, a senior attorney at Environmental Defense, who believed that the expansion of right-to-know programmes would create effective incentives for companies to reduce toxic chemical releases. The overall goal of Score Card, therefore, is to mobilise

information and influence decision making along the entire government–citizens, producer–consumers, and local–national spectrum.

Environmental Defense considers that the biggest impact of Score Card has been to compel the chemical industry to accelerate its testing programmes for basic toxicity data on all high-production chemicals. The chemical industry, of course, has reacted by setting up its own website called www.chemicalguide.com, which also purports to profile chemical facilities, but is, according to Pease, nothing but a "propaganda publication system" (Schienke, 2001, p 3).

Score Card has had impacts in areas that neither Pease nor Environmental Defense expected. In particular, national and local press and media have used information provided on scorecard.org to write local pollution stories, which in turn has brought pressure to bear on both producers and state/federal government. In addition, the website has attracted the interest of a diverse group of people, from teachers, to homebuyers and health professionals. For example, Chris Leporini (2002) claims that Score Card can help house buyers evaluate an area's environmental safety before making the moving decision, and allow house sellers to check before listing a 'toxic home' that could then expose them to liability.

Now that we have a broad overview of IBNIS and some more in-depth understanding of these four examples, we can turn our attention towards how we might begin to theorise their emergence.

Some theoretical perspectives

This chapter reviews a range of research literature that offers analyses of the interface between the internet and urban policy in a manner that provides a useful contextualisation of the emergence of internet-based neighbourhood information systems (IBNIS).

It is only very recently that these two rather different strands of academic literature have begun to engage with one another. Academic studies of the patterns of growth and nature of the social uptake of internet usage have mushroomed over the past decade, but, in their enthusiasm to capture the nature of the *information age*, these studies did not immediately take account of existing neighbourhood and urban research. Conversely, the work of urban sociologists and geographers remained fairly fixed in the 'physical' world of urban social divisions, planning and so on, and did not examine the potential impact of the internet and 'informatisation processes' on urban networks (Burrows and Ellison, 2004). The gap between these different areas of study led the social geographer Steven Graham (2002) to make a programmatic call for new research that is better able to consider the *relationship* between physical urban spaces and the digital technologies that are becoming increasingly important in how these spaces are economically, socially and politically configured.

This, of course, is a huge research agenda, although a good deal of progress has been made in the past few years, not least by Graham himself (Graham, 2004). Even so, a lot remains to be done. Our focus on the emergence of IBNIS should be seen in this context and this report contributes to the agenda by showing that developments in online information systems are not only beginning to filter into the public realm, but that they are doing so in ways that are likely to have consequences for 'real people on the ground'.

Although the global, regional and national statistics on internet use are of interest, as we have already indicated, it is important to understand how the technology is impinging upon everyday practices and with what consequences. Perhaps most progress in showing how this might be happening has been in the area of health research (Nettleton, 2004). In a situation where (in the US at least) "more people go online for medical advice on any given day than actually visit health professionals" (Fox and Rainie, 2002, p 4), it has been impossible to ignore the impact of the online technologies. IBNIS is a similar step-change. Local information, which was previously difficult to collect and collate, is now easily available online – and, of course, it is this explosion of accessible and understandable data at neighbourhood level that has ensured that research on the nature and impact of the internet, and urban studies research, are beginning to come together. One instance of this developing relationship is the growing interest in, and concern about, the role that *software* now plays in urban life.

Software sorted cities?

Although their terminology may be convoluted, there can be no doubt about the importance that Thrift and French (2002, p 309) attach to the role of software in contemporary societies, which they claim increasingly functions to provide a "new and complex form of automated spatiality ... which has important consequences for what we regard as the world's phenomenality".

This notion of 'automated spatiality' simply means that urban places in particular are being 'sorted out' in quite profound ways – not by human beings but by technologically driven processes in which ever more sophisticated software 'fixes' and 'positions' individuals as they go about their daily lives. As Amin and Thrift (2002, pp 43-5) point out:

> ... the city is being fixed, positioned, guided as never before. The map, the census, postcodes, area codes, license plates and other means of producing location have been joined to technologies like GIS, global positioning systems and so on ... to produce spatial categorisations, so that the portion of human subjects dwelling in databases becomes increasingly determinate.

One implication of these processes is that they are beginning actively to structure (and restructure) the places we inhabit in vital, but often unseen, ways (Forrest, 2003). Far from rendering real, physical places unimportant (the so-called 'end of geography' argument), the opposite is the case: digital media, which can appear remote from the immediacies of everyday life, may be having an increasingly tangible impact on how we are sorted – or 'segmented' – in terms of lifestyles, patterns of consumption and, of course, the neighbourhoods in which we live. In other words, these systems are beginning to categorise and define us in ways that may be useful for commercial companies and governments but that might not accord with our perceptions either of ourselves or of our communities. Just as significantly, it is far from clear whether we even *know* that we are subject to these various sorting processes.

This point can be seen most clearly in recent debates about the *digital divide*. We referred to this concept in Chapter 1 in the way it has traditionally been employed – the conviction that the spread of connection to digital information is socially uneven. Basically, so the argument goes, some people can access digital technologies more easily than others. This observation, coupled with the assumption that, *ceteris paribus*, the 'information rich' tend to achieve better outcomes than the 'information poor', has often led to a widespread policy concern to widen access to information and communication technologies (ICTs) – this is a significant dimension of e-government initiatives in recent years. But circumstances have changed. In an environment where the majority of the population in 'Euro-American societies' have internet access, debates about the digital divide have recently widened to encompass concerns about how the online population varies in terms of their differential *utilisation* of digital resources. This has led to the emergence of a second model of the digital divide – one that is as much concerned with issues of people's different capacities both to interpret and then act on information as it is with the socio-structural inequalities of access *per se* (Nettleton and Burrows, 2003; Nettleton et al, 2004).

Graham has proposed a third model, however, which focuses not so much on individuals' abilities to understand and act upon the information they receive, as on the ways in which digital technologies themselves increasingly function to divide populations. This very different conception of the digital divide is particularly relevant to this report because it points to the fact that the ability of social groups and communities to possess or access technology may be less important *than the capacity of technology itself to classify and sort populations*.

Graham accepts, of course, that consumer-citizens have long been sorted and prioritised by a variety of public and private institutions. After all, state welfare agencies like the UK's National Health Service have 'rationed' medical services according to need, length of time on waiting lists, age and so on for well over a generation. But Graham argues that, under the conditions of the information age:

> ... such practices are augmented, or replaced ... by ... software-based techniques, linked to computer databases ... [that] sort users ... work automatically ... continually ... and in real time.
> (Graham, 2004, p 325)

His suggestion is that the surveillance and monitoring capacities of ICTs are being shaped in two related ways, first, to prioritise and enhance the social and structural position, and capacity for social mobility, of certain groups and, second, to add 'friction', barriers and costs to the social position, mobility and opportunities of others. As Graham suggests, this software sorting is:

... being done to overcome problems of congestion, queuing ... and to maximise the quality of service ... for premium privileged users ... ICT-based sorting can allow enhanced functionality to be offered to those deemed attractive ... [whilst] ... less attractive users and communities ... can be pushed away electronically. (2004, p 325)

However, the 'software sorting' technologies that Graham discusses are of two rather different types. On the one hand, some rely upon the actual *physical presence* of software code that affects and acts upon human conduct (Thrift and French, 2002). This is the sense in which Amin and Thrift, following Mitchell (1995, 2000, 2003), argue that in a very material sense software is now just as much a part of the physical fabric of our lives as are bricks, mortar, glass and steel. They write that:

> ... the modern city exists as a haze of software instructions. Nearly every urban practice is becoming mediated by code. There are more lines of code in some modern elevator systems than there were in Apollo spacecraft. (Amin and Thrift, 2002, p 125)

In short, many human activities in contemporary societies depend on coded information that literally enables people to go about their daily lives. Indeed, its absence would bring many essential activities to a halt. But technologies such as 'geodemographic sorting' are different. They are based on procedures that are less proximate and not primarily designed to facilitate the organisation of daily life. Rather, they can be viewed as *new technologies of surveillance* that involve the creation of what some commentators have termed a 'phenetic fix' (Lyon, 2002a; Phillips and Curry, 2002) on society; technologies that:

> ... capture personal data triggered by human bodies and ... use these abstractions to place people in new social classes of income, attributes, preferences, or offences, in order to influence, manage or control them. (Lyon, 2002a, p 3)

The idea of the 'phenetic fix' is all about *classification* – the myriad ways in which human

practices of all kinds, and human beings themselves, can be categorised. The ability to 'segment' populations geodemographically is just another way of dividing up human societies – but it is a particularly powerful one.

Of course, there is nothing new about the phenetic urge (Bowker and Star, 1999), but in the information age this urge to classify has accelerated (Gandy, 1993; Graham, 1998; Haggerty and Ericson, 2000; Staples, 2000; Lyon, 2002a, 2002b, 2003; Elmer, 2004). Widespread processes of sorting, clustering and typifying have come to form a central feature of everyday life. Agents of surveillance no longer need to observe concrete individuals: "much more likely is the creation of categories of interest and classes of conduct thought worthy of attention" (Lyon, 2002a, p 3). Most importantly, the processes of data capture necessary for the creation of these categories are, according to Rose (1999, p 234), increasingly "'designed in' to the flows of everyday life". As Lianos (2003) suggests, however, the growth of such technologies should not necessarily be viewed as deliberate forms of oppressive control. There is, needless to say, no conspiracy here. Rather, a key driver of such developments tends to be the growing commercial preoccupation with the smooth flow of objects, goods and services in the context of a densely 'networked' society. Even so, for Lianos, these technologies are indicative of the decline of traditional forms of collective sociality – for example, the stress on 'community' and the importance of the public sphere – and the creation of new forms of commercialised sociality, increasingly governed by rules of automated flow (cf Thrift and French, 2002).

In light of the above, it was important to gain an understanding of how some of the organisations examined in this report perceive their role in the provision of IBNIS. Is it the case, for instance, that those who build the extraordinarily sophisticated software for geodemographic information systems like PRIZM or MOSAIC have a sense of, and are interested in, the social implications that the widespread use of this data could have as they increasingly permeate the public digital realm? And are those commercial companies that are most closely involved with providing IBNIS services on the 'front line' aware of the ways in which the impact of their activities are being characterised in this research literature? Indeed, are they in fact contributing to the software sorting of neighbourhoods and their populations? Are we entering an era in which software is not only being used by commerce and policy makers to 'sort places out' but is now also being made available to members of the public with the consequence that they can also 'sort themselves out' (Burrows and Ellison, 2004)? At a time when neighbourhoods are becoming more and more homogeneous *within* themselves and more and more heterogeneous *between* themselves (Dorling and Rees, 2003; Dorling and Thomas, 2004), is it recognised that the processes 'on the ground' that are generating such a patterning may be aided and abetted by IBNIS which provides ever better local knowledge about 'where to locate'?

5

Key stakeholder perspectives

A number of individuals were interviewed during the course of this project in both the UK and the USA[6]. These ranged from academics with an interest in online technologies and the potential social implications of digitising information on and about neighbourhoods to representatives of two different types of agency: those private companies that provide data and software services principally for marketing purposes, and other agencies – both private and public sector – that make online information about 'place' available both to corporate users and individual customers. Because one of the objectives of the research was to investigate the potential 'impact of online information on housing and neighbourhood issues', a small number of house buyers were also contacted in order to discover whether they had used online information to facilitate their neighbourhood and property search[7]. What follows summarises the key findings from the interviews conducted in the UK and the US, the information gathered from the US being used as a means of comparing current and future developments in the two countries.

Some key challenges and core issues

Characterising place

Following from the distinctions between the various providers of IBNIS made at the beginning of this report, there is a difference between the approaches to neighbourhood information adopted by companies engaged in software design, primarily for marketing purposes, and those companies that have greater exposure to the public. In the case of the former, while they are obviously careful to characterise segments in ways that are not pejorative, it is the case nevertheless that they have to make meaningful judgements about areas and populations if their information is to be useful to marketers. So, although descriptions of particular localities can be euphemistic, it is hard to avoid labelling areas – and increasingly households – in less than flattering terms. There is some distinction between the UK and US here. In the latter case, Claritas' $PRIZM_{NE}$ package divides US consumers into 15 groups and 62 segments – but the language used to describe segments such as 'big city blues' or 'low-rise living' is not over-colourful. The descriptions associated with MOSAIC's 'welfare borderline' or 'twilight subsistence' categories (see Appendix) are perhaps rather more direct[8].

As we have already mentioned, software developers are alive to the fact that their clustering methodologies will result in segments that are, to an extent, statistical artefacts. The interviews confirmed the fact that extensive

---

[6] In total we interviewed 20 people. These were extraordinary 'interviews as conversations'. Our aim was to 'scope' the nature and potential consequences of IBNIS and, as such, our sample was not necessarily 'representative' of all stakeholders and users. Our aim was to discuss issues with people who appeared to us to be making major contributions to the field from a range of setttings and standpoints. In what follows we do not attach comments to any individuals but, instead, try to offer a schematic summary of the main issues and perspectives that emerged.

[7] Most were recruited following a request on the Radio 4 *Thinking Allowed* programme for people who had used IBNIS for residential search to contact us – the programme can be heard at www.bbc.co.uk/radio4/factual/thinkingallowed_20031001.shtml

[8] Although, interestingly, as yet – unlike ACORN – they are not available through any IBNIS.

efforts are made to reduce potential mis-characterisation by supplementing quantitative data with a range of material – including pictures and detailed qualitative description – that provide a more rounded depiction of a neighbourhood.

The desire to be as accurate as possible when describing places is reflected in the fact that commercial internet companies offering IBNIS to the general public tend to be circumspect in the ways they describe places. While there is obviously interplay between information derived from geodemographic software such as ACORN and PRIZM, these companies take care to ensure that information from other sources – government statistics in the UK, for instance – is available in addition to that contained within geodemographic classifications. There is naturally some overlap here because geodemographic information itself comprises data derived from a range of sources including official statistics. However, there is no doubt that this information is nested within – and contextualised by – other types of data presented by commercial internet companies. So, while ACORN profiles, for example, may be used as a means of providing a general characterisation of a postcode area, it was pointed out that alternative sources of information are also made available. Typically, these are just 'presented' and not 'interpreted' or characterised in the manner of geodemographic information. These 'direct' data will include crime and policing profiles, with the information being drawn from official sources such as the Office for National Statistics (ONS), basic demographic information drawn directly from the Census and a variety of other data about transport, education, local services, pollution levels and so on.

Information accuracy and the problem of 'complaints'

The above suggests that there is a general concern about the accuracy with which places are characterised. Here the distinction between geodemographic software developers and front-line IBNIS companies is replicated. There is some evidence to indicate that geodemographic classification providers – to whom can be added providers of any information who are not themselves likely to be the *direct* object of criticism by those who could potentially feel misrepresented – are rather less concerned than others about how their characterisations of place

could impact on inhabitants. Their main goal, after all, is to develop accurate information for marketers, not for the general public or those inhabiting particular neighbourhoods. One view expressed by an independent data provider in the US was that where cities scored low on his 'best cities' index, this knowledge appeared to spur them into action to promote policies designed to increase their rating. While this observation is important, cities are not 'neighbourhoods' and policy makers – as well as inhabitants themselves – are likely to react differently to information targeted at different geographical levels. Although it is certainly possible that city-wide information can be damaging, as the recent UK publication *Crap towns I and II* (and the associated website noted in Chapter 2) have demonstrated, a positive policy response is perhaps equally likely at this level. However, responses to 'adverse' information will become more sensitive, even hostile, when targeted at even smaller geographical levels. Essentially, the 'closer to home' things get, the greater the danger that people will complain about the characterisation of 'their' neighbourhood.

It is not surprising, then, that commercial internet companies that interface directly with the public are wary about potential inaccuracies and the problems that they might cause. Although the actual numbers of complaints appear to be small – one UK company talked of having 175,000 hits on its geodemographics section in the first month of operation but only 27 complaints – there is no doubt that these companies have neither the time nor the resources to deal with large numbers of complainants. In the US, although there is some evidence to suggest that communities that believe themselves to have been 'informationally misrepresented' are capable of complaining vociferously (even to the point of threatening legal action against those who have drawn up the profiles), the nature of the relationship between front-line companies like Home Store and the general public means that it is unlikely that difficulties of this kind will be widely experienced. This is because companies like Home Store or Find Your Spot have close relationships with realtors. Indeed, as we have seen, in the case of Home Store, the website grew organically from www.realtor.com, the official site of the National Association of Realtors, while Find Your Spot is actually owned by a realtor. In one way or another, then, internet companies of this kind in the US act as conduits putting prospective buyers in touch with realtors, through the medium of neighbourhood information but, importantly, a range of other services as well. Naturally, they are careful to characterise neighbourhoods in an unoffensive manner because they obviously do not want to compromise potential property sales.

The situation is rather different in the UK, although companies appear to be no less cautious about the information they provide. Commercial companies see themselves as providing a service, not so much to estate agents, which keep them at arm's length, but to the general public. This service is aimed at helping consumers make decisions about neighbourhoods in terms of house buying, but also simply to provide useful information (as one developer acknowledged, there are reasons to want to know about the character of neighbourhoods other than wanting to buy property). The significance of property values in the UK is not in doubt, of course, and it is not surprising that wariness about placing inaccurate information on websites that could lead to an unwarranted fall in a neighbourhood's house prices is acute. For this reason, those sites that carry ACORN profiles make it clear that such profiles relate to *patterns of consumption and consumer behaviour* rather than to the character of areas themselves. Again, companies are cautious about taking pay check data down to postcode level, partly because of the danger of inaccuracies, but also because it is not in the interest of commercial internet companies to make people feel bad about their local area.

Environmental information is another case in point, although here data in the UK are shortly to become not just publicly available but probably also a feature of the new 'seller's packs' that vendors may shortly be expected to provide for would-be purchasers. There is an obvious degree of nervousness about this issue – especially perhaps with regard to information about areas likely to be affected by flooding, subsidence or the presence of airborne and other industrial pollutants – and the interviews suggested that a number of commercial companies will be working together to provide information of this kind.

Obtaining relevant information

This set of issues relates to perceived difficulties in getting particular types of data. Although geodemographic classification providers and exposed companies alike have access to a broad range of data compiled from a variety of sources, certain information is hard to come by. Of particular significance are data relating to schools – in both the UK and the US. One UK interviewee commented that school catchment data was the 'Holy Grail' of neighbourhood information because, certainly in the UK context, schools' performance is a leading reason why prospective house buyers choose to move to one area as opposed to another – with these decisions having an impact on property prices. Official websites in the UK – the ONS site, for example – provide data relating to school performance at ward level and it is possible to compare information across wards, although this is not made particularly easy. In the US, government information goes down to city level, where it is possible to obtain data about expenditure per pupil, pupil–teacher ratios and so on.

In the opinion of one software developer, there are no insuperable technological impediments to obtaining detailed comparative data about schools, although there may be dangers in making such information freely available. It appears that the UK government already possesses datasets containing the postcodes of all children at school and, of course, the postcodes of the schools themselves. It would not be difficult to overlay this information with codes from, say, MOSAIC or ACORN that would generate not only richer data about the schools themselves but also the MOSAIC or ACORN profile of every child at a particular school. The dilemma, though, is whether it is considered acceptable that consumers could look up a school in order to discover the kind of pupils that go there – and it is over issues like this that the ambivalence about online information is at its most acute. Companies want to use such information because of the commercial edge it could give them and also, too, because there is a basic belief that members of the public have a right to it. Nevertheless, there is a real awareness of the potential social risks involved in making particular types of information widely available.

A rather easier issue in terms of 'relevance' is environmental information. This appears to be relatively simple to find in the UK, with companies like Home Check providing an internet service at postcode level based on data derived from government sources. In the US, Score Card acts as a social software agency, using information about pollution and environmental hazard derived from the Environmental Protection Agency among other sources. It is not clear, however, how easy environmental information is to come by, or even how widely disseminated it is. One interviewee based in a large company providing IBNIS was unsure about whether online environmental information exists in the US in user-friendly form. Looking beyond the environment, companies like Up My Street want to expand the amount of factual (as opposed to 'judgemental') information wherever possible. Health and transport are considered to be particularly important, although, in the UK at least, the relative paucity of good national databases for these areas is currently making it difficult to provide anything more than the basic information about location and distance from the chosen postcode.

Interactive capability?

Currently IBNIS providers in the UK have no facility for allowing visitors to their websites to customise information. In the US, on the other hand, it is possible for individuals to use websites interactively to prioritise preferred neighbourhood characteristics within a particular city and receive information about which zip codes match this customised profile most closely. Interviews with UK residents engaged in residential search suggested that this capability would be very welcome. Those using UK IBNIS voiced a sense of frustration that they had to triangulate so much information via postcode searches rather than being able to search postcodes by the various characteristics they were seeking. When talking to UK website providers, it was clear that this 'bottom-up' approach to neighbourhood information is something that they would welcome – and something which may not be too long in coming because there is no technological reason to prevent it, as a software developer made clear. However, currently, the only service that even approximates to this consumer-led facility is the 'conversations' type of provision available from

Up My Street, which allows individuals to post opinions, information and so on about local areas and others to respond in threaded discussions. Up My Street is contemplating enhancing this service by organising conversations by category (education, transport and so on) – but this is some way from the more obviously interactive content available in the US.

User-friendliness

Whether talking to software developers themselves, private companies or public sector agencies, the user-friendliness of websites is considered an important issue. Clearly, software developers, or companies like CACI that provide a range of data services, need to develop and/or market packages that can be deployed by intelligent non-specialists who are interested in obtaining particular types of information. It was pointed out in one interview that even commercial companies that could be expected to *want* to manipulate area data themselves for their own ends often expressed no interest in doing so, making it all the more important that sites are easily navigable. Conversely, one software developer expressed the view that the interest in geodemographic information outside the marketing environment had started because employees in the workplace had begun to see the potential of the software for non-commercial purposes. In this individual's opinion, a core factor that dictated this transition from workplace to home was the user-friendliness of the software involved. While it is obvious that companies of all kinds, including public sector providers of statistical data, are concerned about the user-friendliness of their websites, it is equally clear that many sites are not as friendly as they could be. In this regard, a US site acknowledged that its neighbourhood search facility was not particularly easy to access, while one of the UK companies recognised that a feature that ought to be straightforward – the ability to juxtapose postcode information so as to compare different areas on the screen – involved procedures that are more complicated than they need to be.

'Straightforwardness' is particularly important for members of the public, who are visiting sites like Home Store and Up My Street in growing numbers. There is dissimilarity between the US and the UK here. In the US, it appears, IBNIS is still used by members of the public primarily for choosing *properties* – the 'neighbourhood' is a secondary feature. In the UK, however, where property is rapidly becoming the 'new stock market', website users increasingly want to be sure that the neighbourhood in which a prospective property is located will sustain – and indeed increase – the price of the house. Consequently, house buyers want online neighbourhood information that maximises 'searchability' – that is, the capacity to make meaningful comparisons among a number of different localities. Of course, users do not perceive this facility as a *substitute* for some of the traditional activities associated with 'house hunting', but they do perceive IBNIS as a potential 'short cut' around some of the more labour-intensive and time-consuming elements of neighbourhood and property search. To this end, the need is for easily accessible and easily negotiated sites that collate (or allow users to collate) a range of information from different sources with relatively few clicks of the mouse.

Future possibilities and prospects

An important dimension of this study concerns the likely development of online neighbourhood information over the next five to ten years. How did the interviewees perceive the future? For the sake of ease, the responses can be divided into two simple categories. Optimists believe that IBNIS are not only here to stay but will become increasingly important as members of the public become more familiar with the services they provide. Pessimists, conversely, are less sure about the future of IBNIS, although for very different reasons.

Optimism

One view expressed consistently across companies and countries is that efforts will continue to be made to make area information increasingly 'colourful' – and this despite the wariness about making value judgements about particular places. There is a desire to become more user-friendly, as noted, and a corresponding desire to make information available at different levels of geography. As a software developer pointed out, different geographies are required for different purposes. Postcode data will not necessarily be appropriate for agencies that need information about, say,

educational provision in a local education authority area – while, when it comes to the police attempting to protect particular groups against defined risks (for example, older people confronted by individuals impersonating social workers), then the increased detail of these data would be more important. In the future, it was thought that the ability to move among these geographies would become easier, allowing both commercial interests and members of the public to access an increasing diversity of information at the touch of a button.

There is no doubt that information is constantly becoming more detailed and available on ever smaller geographical scales. Software, particularly of the kind that allows visitors to use maps to zoom in and out of different spaces, with levels and types of information changing accordingly, is becoming commonplace. The recent introduction of 'super output areas' (see p 22) by the Office for National Statistics allows website visitors to move between a range of different population sizes and geographies depending on their needs and interests. These are generally perceived as positive developments, bringing greater amounts of information into the public realm.

The increase in a rather different type of 'information' was also predicted, particularly by UK interviewees. This refers to the 'conversations' dimension of sites like Up My Street. It is not difficult to envisage these conversations turning into virtual 'village noticeboards' that would allow a much greater 'community effect' than at present. This would be one step towards allowing people to compare and contrast data of very different kinds – from formal statistical data down to 'unofficial' individual perceptions of place. While elements of this range of information are available today, the real departure would be to get it systematised through one portal that would allow individuals to compare and contrast areas in terms of different geographies and different (subjective) perceptions of place. In this way, the increased digitisation of information on neighbourhoods would, in the view of one interviewee, be the best way of helping consumers towards a final decision about where to live.

Pessimism

Some opinions were expressed that stand in distinct contrast to the above. Certain interviewees – mainly in the US – were less sure about the significance of future developments at *neighbourhood* level. In one case, although an increase in usage of this type of information was predicted, it was also felt that 'neighbourhood search' would remain less important than *property* search. At the very most, online facilities of the kind provided by Find My Spot would help to shorten the time that individuals spend on searching for houses. This insight, though significant, is not 'dramatic'. On this reading, the availability of online neighbourhood information will take its place alongside the traditional activities associated with home buying but will not dominate, for example, the clearly important relationships between purchasers and realtors that exist in the US.

A different form of 'pessimism' is expressed in the view that, in some ways, the era of digitising information on neighbourhoods may already be coming to a close. As we have seen, technological developments mean that it is becoming increasingly possible to focus down ever more closely on the individual household and even the individual consumers within that household ('rooftop level data'). The fact that consumers leave 'traces' wherever they go allows companies to target them as individuals, irrespective of where they live. Contrary to the statement on the Claritas website that 'we are where we live', it may be that online technologies will shortly transform individuals into simply being 'what they consume' – their 'identities' being ascribed accordingly. Aspects of this issue will be taken up in Chapter 6.

Not surprisingly, this view was not endorsed by many interviewees – this no doubt being a function of their involvement in the neighbourhood and property information business. In fact, they displayed a marked lack of interest in one technology that literally 'traces' individual consumers (see, for example, www.followus.co.uk, which allows a registered mobile phone to be tracked). When asked about the potential for G3 mobile phones to be used as mobile providers of consumer and locational information, allowing individuals moving around urban spaces literally to be put in contact with local commercial (and other) facilities,

interviewees were not interested in providing services of this kind nor convinced that individuals themselves wanted them.

6

Conclusions and implications for policy

Theory, practice and the role of IBNIS

If there is one main 'conclusion' to this report, it is that software-based information is very much 'out there' and is being used to 'sort' places and the people who live in them in particular ways. Not only this, but internet-based neighbourhood information systems (IBNIS) are becoming ever more sophisticated and the ability to move among different geographies at different degrees of detail is becoming easier as both the software and associated websites are constantly improved. But are IBNIS a 'good thing'? What are their advantages and disadvantages? Further, as these technologies develop, what kind of policy framework should be created to contain some of the more problematic 'digitally divisive' elements identified by Graham and discussed in Chapter 4? These questions will be considered in this brief final chapter.

The advantages and disadvantages of IBNIS

Software developers and front-line providers clearly believe that they have rich information that is valued not only by commercial operators but also increasingly by the public at large. While front-line companies are understandably wary of presenting 'unadulterated' geodemographic information on their websites, these companies nevertheless epitomise the contemporary urge to *classify*. Although this phenomenon has been a deeply embedded characteristic of all human societies, it is obviously much enhanced by the fact that data gathering and software techniques have arrived at a point where large amounts of complex data about neighbourhoods and the habits and lifestyles of the individuals who live in them are readily available. Little wonder, then, that IBNIS providers are excited by the power of

these technologies and regard them as a good in their own right. Of course, the sheer volume of information about localities is not necessarily an advantage in its own right – but, if such knowledge is both easily accessible and easy to understand, there is reason to believe that it could lead to more sophisticated flows of information about 'who we are and where we live'. In short, there is a prospect that the possession of detailed 'local knowledge' could facilitate various forms of engagement in neighbourhoods – whether this is construed in terms of house buying or local social politics.

A second advantage concerns how ordinary information users could benefit from the detailed online data provided by geodemographic systems and other sources. It is clear from this report that individuals can obtain useful information about areas they live in or areas to which they may want to move with increasing ease. This is a significant new 'service' in an ever more service-oriented society and one that plainly supplements the 'physical' local knowledge that house buyers, parents and others will still need to access. At the very least, IBNIS provide a way of short-cutting some of the more laborious aspects of property search, enabling house purchasers to locate potentially desirable neighbourhoods more easily. However, it is important to remember that IBNIS are not simply about property purchase and that online information can be used for a variety of reasons. For example, IBNIS could be used as a means of risk reduction, providing information about a particular area before a decision is taken to visit it. More positively, online information could benefit certain neighbourhoods by increasing the spread of interest in them: a sort of 'online local tourism' that could lead to enhanced commercial and social activity in the physical world as knowledge about particular venues – pubs, clubs, local facilities and so on – becomes more widely disseminated.

Third, online depictions of particular neighbourhoods could have knock-on effects in terms of local social politics. As the depth and spread of information increases, and it becomes possible to compare different places interactively, so knowledge about how other spaces are organised (or organise themselves) could lead individuals to change particular aspects of their locality. The development of neighbourhood watch schemes, local demands about the lack of particular facilities and public transport issues are just some examples of how information relating to how people live elsewhere could 'feed back' in ways that could enhance the quality of neighbourhood life.

Turning to the disadvantages of IBNIS, it is possible to invert some of the advantages just mentioned to argue, for instance, that the wealth of information that is now available about certain neighbourhoods may not be particularly welcome to those who live in them for the reasons that Graham and others suggest. At one level, the way in which commercial companies target recipients of junk mail or cold calls is often resented and regarded as intrusive. Second, and more importantly, because the sources of geodemographic information and segmentation methodologies are mysterious and not understood by the general public, local residents are unlikely to know how information about their neighbourhood is compiled. This lack of transparency is significant because it compounds the sorting processes present in Graham's 'third dimension' of the digital divide discussed in Chapter 4. Irrespective of front-line companies' own concerns about mis-characterising localities, in an environment in which local residents themselves do not understand how information about their neighbourhoods is being used, they cannot dispute it and so cannot control the uses to which it may be put. The result, in certain areas, could be an inaccurate depiction of place that arguably could lead to unwarranted 'red-lining' with little prospect of challenging the image that has been imposed.

A third disadvantage refers not to the unwarranted ascription of specific characteristics to particular neighbourhoods but to the pejorative descriptions used to convey, however

accurately, images of poverty and deprivation. Such descriptions are likely to contribute to ongoing processes of inter-neighbourhood segregation and intra-neighbourhood homogenisation. It is important to question the desirability of making available information that can undermine the social life and well-being of particular localities. The obverse of 'online tourism' and its potentially beneficial effects on local life is 'online marginalisation' – the virtual segregation of deprived areas.

A policy framework for IBNIS

Allowing for the enormous difficulties involved in 'un-inventing' IBNIS (let alone the 'phenetic urge' of which they are so potent a symbol), the core policy issue to come out of this report is how best to ensure that the advantages of IBNIS are not outweighed by the disadvantages listed above. The key challenge is how to move towards a position in which freely flowing local knowledge can be utilised equitably by all those who wish to benefit from it without having a detrimental impact on neighbourhoods and those who live in them. How, in other words, can processes of software sorting that, by definition, segregate and stratify be 'redeployed' to produce not just accurate information but more democratically accountable depictions of place? There are four main possibilities here:

1. Websites of front-line companies could be required to have easily accessible spaces where local residents can challenge received images of their neighbourhoods. Some companies already provide 'conversations-style' options, which allow individuals to conduct more 'informal' discussions about the merits and demerits of localities, and these are to be encouraged. However, these options are not a substitute for a formal 'neighbourhood responses' page where residents are invited either to challenge or endorse IBNIS characterisations.
2. Companies using geodemographic software should be required to make their sources of local information explicit. 'Sources' here refers both to the enterprise that furnished the geodemographic information *and* how such information was compiled.
3. Alternative websites producing local information need to be encouraged, if necessary with help from public funds. Such

sites could fulfil two key roles. First, by promoting local 'conversations', they would work as virtual noticeboards, which, among other things, would allow local residents (and others) the opportunity to challenge attempts to 'sort them out'. Second, local websites could fulfil a 'social software' role, providing residents with the chance to develop ideas, stimulated by IBNIS characterisations – accurate or inaccurate – about how to improve neighbourhood services and amenities.

4. As IBNIS become increasingly sophisticated, the issue of privacy becomes ever more important. This issue is not specifically about *individual* privacy as much as 'aggregate' or 'collective' privacy – what information it is appropriate to hold on the consumption habits and lifestyles of postcode-size populations, how far it should be permissible to characterise these populations in particular ways and the penalties that should be attached to mis-characterisation. A coherent policy framework should include this dimension as a means of clarifying what is currently an opaque area in which local residents are particularly – and sometimes personally – vulnerable to the consequences of misrepresentation.

5. Local authority departments (social services, housing departments) and other relevant agencies and programmes (such as Job Centres, Sure Start and so on) could be encouraged to be more proactive in making online technologies more freely available. These agencies should make sure that users are aware of IBNIS and how various companies are depicting their neighbourhoods. Individuals should also be informed about alternative websites as described in 3 above.

6. The availability of online resources is not alone sufficient to ensure that local people will be able to use them. As the quantity of local *information* grows, local *knowledge* must keep pace and this requires training and education. With IBNIS only now at the point of take-off, there is a window of opportunity for government and local authorities to develop local training programmes, particularly in vulnerable areas, to provide information about local information and the uses to which it is being put. Local schools may be able to play an important part here, perhaps encouraging children to use IBNIS as part of project work about their local environments.

In outlining this policy framework, one issue has not been addressed. Policies 1 and 3 deal with website matters and clearly demand both access to, and the ability to use, online sources. Although access to the internet has increased dramatically in recent years, as Chapter 1 mentioned, those conceptions of the digital divide discussed in Chapter 4, which relate to the affordability of computer technologies and to individuals' capacity to utilise web-based information effectively, are not, of course, *displaced* by Graham's alternative understanding. Those sections of the population that are financially unable and/or unwilling (as is the case with many older people) to access online sources will be increasingly disadvantaged as information availability and society's dependence on it expands. The problem will be most acute where social demographics and geodemographics interweave – in other words, where deprivation and old age (together with other forms of marginality) are spatially concentrated. In these areas, two additional policies might be required:

References

Abbate, J. (1999) *Inventing the Internet*, Cambridge, MA: MIT Press.

Amin, A. and Thrift, N. (2002) *Cities: Re-imagining the urban*, Oxford: Polity Press.

Bowker, G. and Star, S. (1999) *Sorting things out: Classification and its consequences*, Cambridge, MA: MIT Press.

Burrows, R. and Ellison, N. (2004) 'Sorting places out? Towards a social politics of neighbourhood informatisation', *Information, Communication and Society*, vol 7, no 3, pp 321-36.

Butcher, M. (2003) 'For-sale sign on UpMyStreet.com', *e-consultancy*, www.e-consultancy.com/newsfeatures/newsletter/view.asp?id=640#6803

Castells, M. (2000) *The information age: Economy, society and culture I: The rise of the network society* (2nd edn), Oxford: Blackwell.

Curry, M. (1998) *Digital places: Living with geographic information technologies*, London: Routledge.

Cattell, V. and Evans, M. (1999) *Neighbourhood images in East London: Social capital and social networks on two East London estates*, York: YPS.

Dean, J. and Hastings, A. (2000) *Challenging images: Housing estates, stigma and regeneration*, Bristol: Policy Press.

DigiTV (2004) www.digitv.org.uk/content_images/case_study_somerset_tcm2-441.doc (accessed 6 October 2004).

Dorling, D. and Rees, P.H. (2003) 'A nation still dividing: The British Census and social polarisation 1971-2001', *Environment and Planning A*, vol 35, no 7, pp 1287-313.

Dorling, D. and Thomas, B. (2004) *People and places: A 2001 Census atlas of the UK*, Bristol: The Policy Press.

Elmer, G. (2004) *Profiling machines: Mapping the personal information economy*, Cambridge, MA: MIT Press.

Forrest, R. (2003) 'Who cares About neighbourhoods?', Plenary Paper Housing Studies Association Conference on Community, Neighbourhood, Justice, Bristol, September, www.york.ac.uk/inst/chp/hsa/papers/autumn03/forrest.pdf

Forrest, R. and Kearns, A. (1999) *Joined-up places? Social cohesion and neighbourhood regeneration*, York: YPS.

Fox, S. and Rainie, L. (2002) *Vital decisions*, Pew Internet and American Life Project, Washington, DC: Pew Institute.

Gandy, O. (1993) *The panoptic sort: A political economy of personal information*, Boulder, CO: Westview.

Gibson, O. (2003a) 'Is it the end of the road for UpMyStreet?', *The Guardian*, 4 April 2003.

Gibson, O. (2003b) 'UpMyStreet rescued', *The Guardian*, 15 May 2003.

Goss, J. (1995a) 'We know who you are and we know where you live: the instrumental rationality of geodemographic systems', *Economic Geography*, vol 71, no 2, pp 171-98.

Goss, J. (1995b) 'Marketing the new marketing: the strategic discourses of GIS', in J. Pickles (ed) *Ground truth: The social implications of GIS*, New York, NY: Guilford Press, pp 130-70.

Graham, S. (1998) 'Spaces of surveillant simulation: new technologies, digital representations and material geographies', *Environment and Planning D: Society and Space*, vol 16, no 4, pp 483-504.

Graham, S. (2002) 'Bridging digital divides? Urban polarisations and ICTs', *Urban Studies*, vol 39, no 1, pp 33-56.

Graham, S. (2004) 'The software sorted city: rethinking the "digital divide"', in S. Graham (ed) *The cybercities reader*, London: Routledge, pp 324-31.

Graham, S. and Marvin, S. (2001) *Splintering urbanism: Networked infrastructures, technological mobilities and the urban condition*, London: Routledge.

Haggerty, K. and Ericson, R. (2000) 'The surveillant assemblage', *British Journal of Sociology*, vol 51, no 4, pp 605-20.

Harris, T. and Weiner, D. (eds) (1996) *GIS and society: The social implications of how people, space and environment are represented in GIS*, National Centre for Geographic Information and Analysis, www.geo.wvu.edu/www/i19/page.html

Janes, L. and Mooney, G. (2002) 'Place, lifestyle and social divisions', in P. Braham and L. Janes (eds) *Social differences and divisions*, Oxford: Blackwell, pp 1-57.

Krouk, D., Pitkin, B. and Richman, N. (2000) 'Internet-based neighbourhood information systems: a comparative analysis', in M. Gurstein (ed) *Community informatics: Enabling communities with information and communications technology*, London: Idea Group Publishing, pp 275-97.

Krupp, F. (2004) Letter from Fred Krupp, Executive Director, Environmental Defense, to scorecard.org visitor, www.scorecard.org/about/about-why.tcl (accessed 27 September 2004).

Leporini, C. (2002) 'Get the lowdown on pollution levels, *Realtor Magazine Online*, 3 Jan 2002, www.realtormag.com/rmomag.nsf/pages/website200203041?OpenDocument (accessed 28 September 2004).

Lianos, M. (2003) 'Social control after Foucault', *Surveillance and Society*, vol 1, no 3, www.surveillance-and-society.org.

Lyon, D. (2002a) 'Surveillance studies: understanding visibility, mobility and the phenetic fix', *Surveillance and Society*, vol 1, no 1, www.surveillance-and-society.org.

Lyon, D. (2002b) 'Everyday surveillance: personal data and social classifications', *Information, Communication and Society*, vol 5, no 2, pp 242-57.

Lyon, D. (2003) *Surveillance and social sorting: Privacy, risk and digital discrimination*, London: Routledge.

Mitchell, M.J. (1995) *City of bits*, Cambridge, MA: MIT Press.

Mitchell, M.J. (2000) *E-topia*, Cambridge, MA: MIT Press.

Mitchell, M.J. (2003) *ME++*, Cambridge, MA: MIT Press.

Monmonier, M. (2002) *Spying with maps: Surveillance technologies and the future of privacy*, Chicago, IL: University of Chicago Press.

Nettleton, S. (2004) 'The emergence of e-scaped medicine?', *Sociology*, vol 38, no 4, pp 661-79.

Nettleton, S. and Burrows, R. (2003) 'E-scaped medicine? Information, reflexivity and health', *Critical Social Policy*, vol 23, no 2, pp 165-85.

Nettleton, S., Burrows, R., O'Malley, L. and Watt, I. (2004) '"Health e-types": an analysis of the everyday use of the internet for health', *Information, Communication and Society*, vol 7, no 4, pp 531-53.

Online Publishing News (2002) 'Publisher creates revenue from co-branding', 19 April 2002, www.onlinepublishingnews.com/htm/n20020419.294672.htm (accessed 28 September 2004).

ONS (Office for National Statistics) (2002) *Spring 2002 departmental report*, ONS: London, Crown Copyright.

ONS (2004a) *Neighbourhood statistics: Report to ministers 2001/2003*, ONS: London, Crown Copyright.

ONS (2004b) Neighbourhood Statistics Service, Background, http://neighbourhood.statistics.gov.uk/background_info_rev5.asp (accessed 19 October 2004).

PAT 18 (2000) *Report of the Policy Action Team 18: Better information*, London: Social Exclusion Unit/ODPM, Crown Copyright.

Phillips, D. and Curry, M. (2002) 'Privacy and the phenetic urge: geodemographics and the changing spatiality of local practice', in D. Lyon (ed) *Surveillance as social sorting: Privacy, risk and digital discrimination*, London: Routledge, pp 137-52.

Pickles, J. (ed) (1995) *Ground truth: The social implications of GIS*, New York, NY: Guilford Press.

Price, T. (2000) *Cyber activism: Advocacy groups and the Internet*, Washington, DC: Foundation for Public Affairs.

Rose, N. (1999) *Powers of freedom*, Cambridge, MA: Cambridge University Press.

Schienke, E. (2001) 'Bill Pease: an original developer of scorecard.org', CECS Working Interviews, Troy, NY: Center for Ethics in Complex Systems, RPI, 17 November.

SEU (Social Exclusion Unit) (1998) *Bringing Britain together: A national strategy for neighbourhood renewal*, Cm 4045, London: Social Exclusion Unit, The Stationery Office.

Silburn, R., Lucas, D., Page, R. and Hanna, L. (2000) *Neighbourhood images in Nottingham: Social cohesion and neighbourhood change*, York: YPS.

Staples, W. (2000) *Everyday surveillance: Vigilance and visibilty in postmodern life*, Lanham, MD: Rowman and Littlefield.

Statistics Commission (2001) Letter to James Denman, Office for National Statistics, from the Statistics Commission Secretariat, 15 August.

Thrift, N. and French, S. (2002) 'The automatic production of space', *Transactions of the Institute of British Geographers*, vol 27, no 4, pp 309-35.

Webber, R. (2004) 'Designing geodemographic classifications to meet contemporary business needs', *Interactive Marketing*, vol 5, no 3, pp 219-37.

Webber, R. and Craig, J. (1976) 'Which local authorities are alike?', *Population Trends*, 5, pp 13-19.

Webber, R. and Craig, J. (1978) *A socio-economic classification of local authorities in Great Britain*, London: HMSO.

Weiss, M. (2000) *The clustered world*, Boston, MA: Little, Brown and Co.

Westwood, S. and Williams, J. (eds) (1997) *Imagining cities: Scripts, signs, memory*, London: Routledge.

Witchells, C. (2003) 'Street plight', *The Guardian*, 14 April.

Wood, M. and Vamplew, C. (1999) *Neighbourhood images in Teesside: Regeneration or decline?*, York: YPS.

Appendix:
ACORN and MOSAIC
geodemographic classifications

Table A.1: The ACORN classification© CACI

Category	Group	Type	%
Wealthy achievers	Wealthy executives	Wealthy mature professionals, large houses	1.7
		Wealthy working families with mortgages	1.5
		Villages with wealthy commuters	2.7
		Well-off managers, larger houses	2.6
	Affluent greys	Older affluent professionals	1.8
		Farming communities	2.0
		Old people, detached homes	1.9
		Mature couples, smaller detached homes	2.0
	Flourishing families	Older families, prosperous suburbs	2.1
		Well-off working families with mortgages	2.3
		Well-off managers, detached houses	3.7
		Large families and houses in rural areas	0.6
Urban prosperity	Prosperous professionals	Well-off professionals, larger houses and converted flats	0.9
		Older professionals in suburban houses and apartments	1.4
	Educated urbanites	Affluent urban professionals, flats	1.1
		Prosperous young professionals, flats	0.9
		Young educated workers, flats	0.6
		Multi-ethnic young, converted flats	1.1
		Suburban privately renting professionals	0.9
	Aspiring singles	Student flats and cosmopolitan sharers	0.6
		Singles and sharers, multi-ethnic areas	1.6
		Low-income singles, small rented flats	1.2
		Student terraces	0.4
Comfortably off	Starting out	Young couples, flats and terraces	1.0
		White-collar singles/sharers, terraces	1.4
	Secure families	Younger white-collar couples with mortgages	1.9
		Middle income, home owning areas	2.9
		Working families with mortgages	2.6
		Mature families in suburban semis	3.3
		Established home owning workers	3.6
		Home owning Asian family areas	1.1
	Settled suburbia	Retired home owners	0.9
		Middle income, older couples	3.0
		Lower incomes, older people, semis	2.1
	Prudent pensioners	Elderly singles, purpose-built flats	0.7
		Older people, flats	1.9

Table A.1: contd.../

Category	Group	Type	%
Moderate means	Asian communities	Crowded Asian terraces	0.5
		Low-income Asian families	1.1
	Post-industrial families	Skilled older families, terraces	2.8
		Young working families	2.1
	Blue-collar roots	Skilled workers, semis and terraces	3.3
		Home owning families, terraces	2.8
		Older people, rented terraces	1.8
Hard-pressed	Struggling families	Low-income larger families, semis	3.3
		Low income, older people, smaller semis	3.0
		Low income, routine jobs, terraces and flats	1.4
		Low-income families, terraced estates	2.6
		Families and single parents, semis and terraces	2.1
		Large families and single parents, many children	1.7
	Burdened singles	Single elderly people, council flats	1.8
		Single parents and pensioners, council terraces	1.9
		Families and single parents, council flats	0.8
	High-rise hardship	Old people, many high-rise flats	0.8
		Singles and single parents, high-rise estates	0.9
	Inner city adversity	Multi-ethnic purpose-built estates	1.1
		Multi-ethnic, crowded flats	1.1
	Unclassified	Mainly communal population	0.3

Table A.2 The MOSAIC classification© Experian

Group description	Type description	%
Symbols of success	Global connections	0.72
	Cultural leadership	0.92
	Corporate chieftains	1.12
	Golden empty nesters	1.33
	Provincial privilege	1.66
	High technologists	1.82
	Semi-rural seclusion	2.04
Happy families	Just moving in	0.91
	Fledgling nurseries	1.18
	Upscale new owners	1.35
	Families making good	2.32
	Middle-rung families	2.86
	Burdened optimists	1.96
	In military quarters	0.17
Suburban comfort	Close to retirement	2.81
	Conservative values	2.84
	Small-time business	2.93
	Sprawling subtopia	3.08
	Original suburbs	2.41
	Asian enterprise	1.02
Ties of community	Respectable rows	2.65
	Affluent blue collar	3.12
	Industrial grit	3.82
	Coronation street	2.81
	Town centre refuge	1.13
	South Asian industry	0.88
	Settled minorities	1.62
Urban intelligence	Counter-cultural mix	1.36
	City adventurers	1.27
	New urban colonists	1.36
	Caring professionals	1.08
	Dinky developments	1.10
	Town gown transition	0.76
	University challenge	0.26
Welfare borderline	Bedsit beneficiaries	0.71
	Metro multiculture	1.67
	Upper floor families	1.72
	Tower block living	0.49
	Dignified dependency	1.34
	Sharing a staircase	0.50
Municipal dependency	Families on benefits	1.21
	Low horizons	2.64
	Ex-industrial legacy	2.86

Table A.2: contd.../

Group description	Type description	%
Blue-collar enterprise	Rustbelt resilience	3.00
	Older right to buy	2.67
	White van culture	3.17
	New town materialism	2.17
Twilight subsistence	Old people in flats	0.83
	Low-income elderly	1.63
	Cared for pensioners	1.43
Grey perspectives	Sepia memories	0.75
	Child-free serenity	1.34
	High-spending elders	1.53
	Bungalow retirement	1.26
	Small town seniors	2.71
	Tourist attendants	0.30
Rural isolation	Summer playgrounds	0.29
	Greenbelt guardians	1.74
	Parochial villagers	1.64
	Pastoral symphony	1.31
	Upland hill farmers	0.41

Also available from The Policy Press

Published in association with the Joseph Rowntree Foundation

Geographcal mobility
Family impacts
Anne E. Green and Angela Canny

This report charts the changing role and nature of geographical mobility in organisational strategies and career development. It explores the work and family life experiences of employees and partners who have faced job-related geographical mobility.

Paperback £13.95 US$23.95 ISBN 1 86134 501 1

297 x 210mm 64 pages May 2003

Family and Work series

Neighbourhoods that work
A study of the Bournville estate, Birmingham
Rick Groves, Alan Middleton, Alan Murie and Kevin Broughton

This study provides the results from major original research addressing issues which are central to current debates about social cohesion and neighbourhood renewal. The research focuses on Bournville - a successful, mixed tenure residential neighbourhood in Birmingham. The findings of the study contribute to current debates about social capital and policy responses designed to achieve more balanced and cohesive neighbourhoods.

Paperback £14.95 US$25.50 ISBN 1 86134 538 0

297 x 210mm 72 pages July 2003

Poverty and home ownership in contemporary Britain
Roger Burrows

"... important reading for policy makers and academics with an interest in housing and social protection." *SPA News*

"This (welcomingly short) report deals with the complexities of poverty definition in very accessible form." *Housing Studies*

This report demonstrates the urgent need to re-evaluate our understanding of both poverty and home ownership. Drawing on data from the Joseph Rowntree Foundation's Poverty and Social Exclusion Survey of Britain, it presents a detailed picture of the realities of home ownership at the margins and provides evidence in support of the need for radical changes in policy towards sustainable home ownership.

Paperback £11.95 US$17.95 ISBN 1 86134 465 1

297 x 210mm 48 pages January 2003

Anti-social behaviour strategies
Finding a balance
Andrew Millie, Jessica Jacobson, Eraina McDonald and Mike Hough

The Government has introduced new powers for tackling anti-social behaviour, such as Anti-Social Behaviour Orders (ASBOs). This study examines how the new powers are being used, and what people think about them. Its findings will advance strategic thinking on the issue.

Paperback £13.95 US$23.95 ISBN 1 86134 763 4

297 x 210mm 72 pages June 2005

FREE pdf version available online at www.jrf.org.uk

Affordable credit
The way forward
Sharon Collard and Elaine Kempson

The poor pay more for many things but, arguably, it is the extra they pay for credit that puts the greatest strain on their budgets. This report looks beyond the rhetoric that has dominated much of the debate on high-cost credit to examine the scope for widening access to more affordable credit.

Paperback £11.95 US$19.95 ISBN 1 86134 687 5

297 x 210mm 48 pages February 2005

FREE pdf version available online at www.jrf.org.uk

What works in assessing community participation?
Danny Burns, Frances Heywood, Pete Wilde and Mandy Wilson

"... very readable and interesting." *LGA update*

This report documents the results of road-testing two frameworks for assessing community participation: *Active partners: Benchmarking community involvement in regeneration* (Yorkshire Forward, 2000) and *Auditing community participation: An assessment handbook* (The Policy Press, 2000).

The report examines whether the tools were useful, what worked most effectively and how the tools might be amalgamated on the basis of what was learned from the road-testing.

Paperback £13.95 US$23.95 ISBN 1 86134 615 8

297 x 210mm 56 pages July 2004

Making community participation meaningful
A handbook for development and assessment
Danny Burns, Frances Heywood, Marilyn Taylor, Pete Wilde and Mandy Wilson

"... a useful handbook for anyone working within their local community." *LGA update*

Community participation is now demanded of virtually all public sector services and programmes. This handbook provides practitioners, community activists, regeneration managers, teachers and academics with the tools needed to ensure that it is effective.

Paperback £14.95 US$25.50 ISBN 1 86134 614 X

297 x 210mm 76 pages July 2004

'Faith' in urban regeneration?
Engaging faith communities in urban regeneration
Richard Farnell, Robert Furbey, Stephen Shams al-Haqq Hills, Marie Macey and Greg Smith

"... will be read with profit by regeneration officials and members of faith communities." *Journal of Social Policy*

Community involvement is seen as essential for successful urban regeneration, but it often proves elusive. The UK government has identified 'faith communities' as an important resource. This report explores the present and potential contribution of religious communities and their members, and the tensions and controversies involved in engaging with 'faith'.

Paperback £13.95 US$23.95 ISBN 1 86134 516 X

297 x 210mm 64 pages April 2003

Schools and area regeneration
Deanne Crowther, Colleen Cummings, Alan Dyson and Alan Millward

This report explores the ways in which schools serving two economically and socially disadvantaged urban areas have attempted to balance their educational aims with growing demands to engage in community life. It focuses on the relationship between the schools and their respective communities and on outcomes in terms of individual and community development.

Paperback £13.95 US$23.95 ISBN 1 86134 517 8

297 x 210mm 64 pages October 2003

Approaches to community governance
Models for mixed tenure communities
Martin Knox, David Alcock, Anna Roderick and John Iles

This report examines what legal mechanisms exist for involving residents across all tenures in having a say in how their neighbourhood is run.

Paperback £13.95 US$20.95 ISBN 1 86134 461 9

297 x 210mm 56 pages November 2002

Best practice in regeneration
Because it works
Tony Trott

This report highlights the key practical themes of successful regeneration - what works and where – and effective ways of learning from the experiences of others.

Paperback £11.95 US$17.95 ISBN 1 86134 455 4

297 x 210mm 32 pages November 2002

To order further copies of this publication or any other Policy Press titles please visit **www.policypress.org.uk** or contact:

In the UK and Europe:
Marston Book Services, PO Box 269, Abingdon, Oxon, OX14 4YN, UK
Tel: +44 (0)1235 465500
Fax: +44 (0)1235 465556
Email: direct.orders@marston.co.uk

In the USA and Canada:
ISBS, 920 NE 58th Street, Suite 300, Portland, OR 97213-3786, USA
Tel: +1 800 944 6190 (toll free)
Fax: +1 503 280 8832
Email: info@isbs.com

In Australia and New Zealand:
DA Information Services, 648 Whitehorse Road Mitcham, Victoria 3132, Australia
Tel: +61 (3) 9210 7777
Fax: +61 (3) 9210 7788
E-mail: service@dadirect.com.au

Further information about all of our titles can be found on our website.